5 New
SAT
MATH PRACTICE TESTS

AMERICAN MATH
ACADEMY

By H. TONG, M.Ed.

Math Instructional & Olympiad Coach

www.americanmathacademy.com

AMERICAN MATH
ACADEMY

5 NEW SAT MATH PRACTICE TESTS

Writer: H.Tong
Copyright © 2019 The American Math Academy LLC.

Printed in United States of America.

ISBN: 9781091573833

SAT is registered trademark of the College Entrance Examination Board, which is not involved in the production of, and does not endorse, this product.

Although the writer has made every effort to ensure the accuracy and completeness of information contained this book, the writer assumes no responsibility for errors, inaccuracies, omissions or any inconsistency herein. Any slighting of people, places, or organizations unintentional.

Questions, suggestions or comments, please email: americanmathacademy@gmail.com

TABLE OF CONTENTS

About the Author

Mr. Tong teaches at various private and public schools in both New York and New Jersey. In conjunction with his teaching, Mr. Tong developed his own private tutoring company. His company developed a unique way of ensuring their students' success on the math section of the SAT. His students, over the years, have been able to apply the knowledge and skills they learned during their tutoring sessions in college and beyond. Mr. Tong's academic accolades make him the best candidate to teach SAT Math. He received his master's degree in Math Education. He has won several national and state championships in various math competitions and has taken his team to victory in the Olympiads. He has trained students for Math Counts, American Math Competition (AMC), Harvard MIT Math Tournament, Princeton Math Contest, and the National Math League, and many other events. His teaching style ensures his students' success—he personally invests energy and time into his students and sees what and what they're struggling with. His dedication towards his students is evident through his students' achievements.

Acknowledgements

I would like to take the time to acknowledge the help and support of my beloved wife, my colleagues, and my students–their feedback on my book was invaluable. I would like to say an additional thank you to my dear friend Robert for his assistance in making this book complete. Without everyone's help, this book would not be the same. I dedicate this book to my precious daughter Vera, my inspiration to take on this project.

SAMPLE SAT MATH QUESTIONS

Question #1

If $3x - ay + 12 = 0$ and the slope of the equation is $\frac{3}{4}$, then what is the value of a?

A) 4

B) $\frac{1}{4}$

C) 2

D) $\frac{1}{2}$

Solution:

$3x - ay + 12 = 0$ and $m = \frac{3}{4}$

Slope of equation : $m = \frac{3}{a}$

$\frac{3}{a} = \frac{3}{4}$, then $a = 4$

Correct Answer : A

Question #2

If $x - 3y = 3$, then find $\frac{2^x}{8^y}$

A) 4

B) 8

C) 16

D) 32

Solution:

$x - 3y = 3$, then $\frac{2^x}{2^{3y}} = 2^{x-3y} = 2^3 = 8$

Correct Answer : B

Question #3

$$x + 3ky = 12$$
$$5x - 12y = 18$$

In the system of equations above, k is a constant. For what value of k will the system of equations have no solutions?

A) $-\frac{4}{5}$

B) $\frac{4}{5}$

C) $\frac{5}{4}$

D) $-\frac{5}{4}$

Solution:

$x + 3ky = 12$

$5x - 12y = 18$

$m_1 = \frac{-1}{3k}$, $m_2 = \frac{+5}{12}$

if a system has no solution,

then slopes must be equals.

$m_1 = m_2$

$\frac{-1}{3k} = \frac{+5}{12}$, $15k = -12$

$k = \frac{-12}{15} = \frac{-4}{5}$

Correct Answer : A

American Math Academy

1

Question #4

$$\frac{3(x+5)-8}{7} = \frac{17-(6-x)}{5}$$

In the equation above, what is the value of x?

A) $\frac{21}{4}$

B) $\frac{11}{4}$

C) $\frac{4}{21}$

D) $\frac{23}{4}$

Solution:

$$\frac{3x+15-8}{7} = \frac{17-6+x}{5}$$

$$\frac{3x+7}{7} = \frac{11+x}{5} \text{(Cross multiply)}$$

$$5(3x+7) = 7(11+x)$$

$$15x+35 = 77+7x$$

$$15x-7x = 77-35$$

$$8x = 42$$

$$x = \frac{42}{8} = \frac{21}{4}$$

Correct Answer : A

Question #5

Simplify $\frac{x^2y+xy^2-xy}{x^2+xy-x}$

A) x

B) y

C) 2xy

D) $-x$

Solution:

$$\frac{x^2y+xy^2-xy}{x^2+xy-x}$$

$$= \frac{xy(x+y-1)}{x(x+y-1)}$$

$$= \frac{xy}{x} = y$$

Correct Answer : B

Question #6

Which of the following is equal to $\frac{8^2 \cdot 16^3}{2^{10}}$?

A) 2^8

B) 2^7

C) 2^5

D) 2^4

Solution:

$$\frac{8^2 \cdot 16^3}{2^{10}} = \frac{2^6 \cdot 2^{12}}{2^{10}} = \frac{2^{18}}{2^{10}} = 2^8$$

Correct Answer : A

Question #7

Mr. Robert is planning to register at Star Fitness. If the center's monthly fee is $25 and $5 per hour, which of following functions gives Mr. Robert the cost, in dollars, for a month in which he spends x hours training?

A) $F(x) = 5x$

B) $F(x) = 25x$

C) $F(x) = 5 + 25x$

D) $F(x) = 25 + 5x$

Solution:

Mounthly Fee $= \$25$

Per hour : $\$5$

Monthly spending : x hours

$F(x) = 25 + 5x$

Correct Answer : D

Question #8

If $x^2 + ax - 10 = (x - 1)(bx + c)$, then find $b + c$.

A) 50

B) 10

C) 11

D) 12

Solution:

$x^2 + ax - 10 = (x-1)(bx + c)$

$x^2 + ax - 10 = bx^2 + cx - bx - c$

$bx^2 = x^2 \quad , \quad b = 1$

$-10 = -c \quad , \quad c = 10$

$b + c = 11$

Correct Answer : C

Question #9

What are the zeros the function $f(x) = x^3 + 8x^2 + 16x$?

A) $0, -2$

B) $0, -3$

C) $0, -4$

D) $0, -5$

Solution:

$f(x) = x^3 + 8x^2 + 16x = 0$

$f(x) = x(x^2 + 8x + 16) = 0$

$f(x) = x(x+4)(x+4) = 0$

$x = 0$ or $x + 4 = 0, x = -4$

Correct Answer : C

Question #10

If the equation $\dfrac{20x^2}{2x-1}$ is written in the form $k+\dfrac{5}{2x-1}$ which of the following gives k in terms of x?

A) $10-5x$

B) $10x+5$

C) $5x+10$

D) $5x-10$

Solution:

$$
\begin{array}{r}
10x+5 \\
2x-1\overline{\smash{\big)}\ 20x^2} \\
\underline{-20x^2 \pm 10x} \\
10x \\
\underline{10x \pm 5} \\
5
\end{array}
$$

$k+\dfrac{5}{2x-1}=10x+5+\dfrac{5}{2x-1}$

$k=10x+5$

Correct Answer : B

Question #11

If a and b are positive integers and $\sqrt{a}=b^2=4$, then which of following is the value of $a-b$?

A) 0

B) 1

C) 12

D) 14

Solution:

$b \mp 2$ since b is positive then

$b=2$

$a=16$

$a-b=16-2=14$

Correct Answer : D

Question #12

If $\dfrac{x+a}{4}=\dfrac{x-a}{3}$, then find a in terms of x.

A) $\dfrac{7}{x}$

B) $\dfrac{x}{7}$

C) $7x$

D) $7-x$

Solution:

$\dfrac{x+a}{4}=\dfrac{x-a}{3}$ (cross multiply)

$4x-4a=3x+3a$

$x=7a$

$\dfrac{x}{7}=a$

Correct Answer : B

Question #13

If P(x + 1) = 3x + 1, then what is P(x + 3)?

A) 2x + 7

B) 3x + 7

C) −3x + 5

D) 2x + 1

Solution:

P(x + 1) = 3x + 1

P(x + 2) + 1) = 3(x + 2) + 1

P(x + 3) = 3x + 6 + 1 = 3x + 7

Correct Answer : B

Question #14

$\dfrac{2x+4}{6} - \dfrac{x}{4} = \dfrac{3}{2}$, find the value of x.

A) 10

B) 12

C) 16

D) 18

Solution:

$$\frac{2x+4}{6} - \frac{x}{4} = \frac{3}{2}$$

$$\frac{4x+8}{12} - \frac{3x}{12} = \frac{18}{12} \text{(cancel denominator)}$$

$$4x + 8 - 3x = 18$$

$$x + 8 = 18$$

$$x = 10$$

Correct Answer : A

Question #15

According to the formula $F = \dfrac{9}{5}C + 32°$, the temperature in degrees Fahrenheit for a given temperature in degrees Celsius C. Find the F when C = 15°.

A) 15°

B) 25°

C) 42°

D) 59°

Solution:

$$F = \frac{9}{5}C + 32° \text{ since } C = 15°$$

$$F = \frac{9}{5}(15°) + 32°$$

$$F = 27° + 32°$$

$$F = 59°$$

Correct Answer : D

American Math Academy

Question #16

If x is a positive integer and $x^2 + x - 20 = 0$, what is the value of $x + 3$?

A) 3

B) 5

C) 7

D) 9

Solution:

$$x^2 + x - 20 = 0$$

$$(x - 4)(x + 5) = 0$$

$$x - 4 = 0, x = 4$$

or

$x + 5 = 0, x = -5$ since x is a positive

integer, it cannot be negative.

$$x + 3 = 4 + 3 = 7$$

Correct Answer : C

Question #17

$$i^0 + i^{31} + i^{10}$$

Which of the following is equivalent to the complex number shown above? ($i^2 = -1$)

A) i

B) $-i$

C) $2i$

D) $-2i$

Solution:

Rule: $i^2 = -1$

$$= i^0 + i^{31} + i^{10}$$

$$= 1 + (i^2)^{15} \cdot i + (i^2)^5$$

$$= 1 + (-1)^{15} \cdot i + (-1)^5$$

$$= 1 - i - 1$$

$$= -i$$

Correct Answer : B

American Math Academy

Question #18

$\dfrac{a^{2m}}{a^{10}} = a^{12}$ and $a^{3n} = a^{21}$, then find $m \cdot n$?

A) 55

B) 66

C) 77

D) 88

Solution:

$\dfrac{a^{2m}}{a^{10}} = a^{12}$ and $a^{3n} = a^{21}$.

$a^{2m} = a^{22}$, then $m = 11$.

$a^{3n} = a^{21}$, then $n = 7$

$m \cdot n = 11 \cdot 7 = 77$

Correct Answer : C

Question #19

Write the equation in slope - intercept form for the line that passes through the points $(-2, 4)$ and $(6, -4)$

Solution:

Slope of two points:

$m = \dfrac{y_2 - y_1}{x_2 - x_1}$

$m = \dfrac{-4 - 4}{6 - (-2)} = \dfrac{-8}{8}$

$m = -1$

$y = mx + b$

use $(-2, 4)$ to find b

$y = mx + b$

$4 = -2(-1) + b$

$4 = 2 + b$

$2 = b$

Correct Answer : $y = -x + 2$

American Math Academy

REFERENCE SHEET

Directions

For each question from 1 to 15, solve each problem, choose the best answer from the choices provided, and fill in the corresponding bubble on your answer sheet.

- For questions 16 to 20, solve the problem and enter your answer in the grid on the answer sheet.

- Refer to the directions before question 18 for how to enter your answers in the grid. You may use any available space for scratch work.

REFERENCE

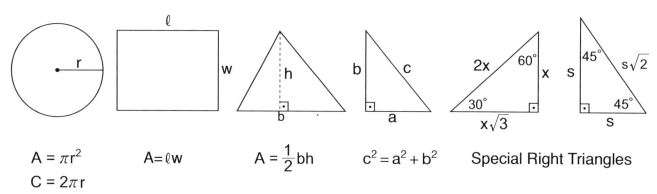

$A = \pi r^2$

$C = 2\pi r$

$A = \ell w$

$A = \frac{1}{2}bh$

$c^2 = a^2 + b^2$

Special Right Triangles

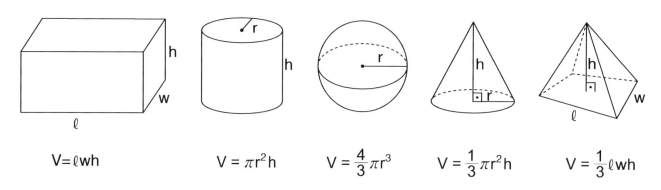

$V = \ell w h$

$V = \pi r^2 h$

$V = \frac{4}{3}\pi r^3$

$V = \frac{1}{3}\pi r^2 h$

$V = \frac{1}{3}\ell w h$

The number of degrees in a circle is 360.

The number of radians in a circle is 2π.

The sum of the measures in degrees of the angles of a triangle is 180.

1.
$$\begin{cases} \dfrac{2}{3}x + \dfrac{3}{4}y = 12 \\ \dfrac{1}{3}x + \dfrac{3}{2}y = 18 \end{cases}$$

In the system of equations above, solve for the y value.

A) 3

B) 32

C) $\dfrac{3}{32}$

D) $\dfrac{32}{3}$

2.
$$x + 2y = 8$$
$$3x - 2y = 12$$

In the system of equations above, what is the value of x+y?

A) 3

B) 13

C) $\dfrac{13}{2}$

D) $\dfrac{2}{13}$

3.
$$(x+3)^2 - 12$$

Which of the following is equivalent to the expression above?

A) $x^2 + 6x - 3$

B) $x^2 + 6x + 3$

C) $x^2 + 3x - 3$

D) $x^2 + 9x + 3$

4.
$$y = mx^2 + 3x + k$$

The graph of the function above has a y −intercept at $y = -2$ and a x−intercept at $x = 2$. What is the value of m?

A) 1

B) 0

C) −1

D) −2

5. Melisa is 6 years younger than twice her sister's age. If Melisa is 24 years old, then how old is Melisa's sister?

A) 12

B) 15

C) 17

D) 21

American Math Academy

6.
$$f(x) = mx^2 + k$$

In the function above, m and k are constants, f (0) = 3, and f (2) = 7. What is the value of $f\left(\dfrac{-1}{2}\right)$?

A) 4

B) 13

C) $\dfrac{13}{4}$

D) $\dfrac{4}{13}$

7. If x and y are positive integers and $\sqrt{x} = y^2 = 9$, then which of following is the value of x − y?

A) 18

B) 27

C) 48

D) 78

8.

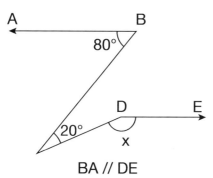

BA // DE

What is the value of x?

A) 70

B) 90

C) 110

D) 120

9.

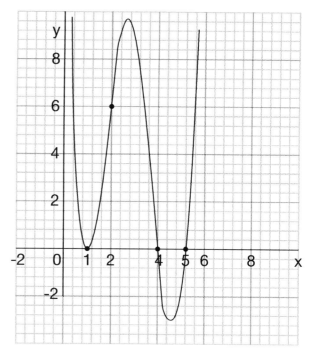

The function y = f (x) is graphed in the xy coordinate plane above. Which of the following equations could describe f (x)?

A) $f(x) = (x - 1)^2 \cdot (x - 4) \cdot (x - 5)$

B) $f(x) = (x + 1)^2 \cdot (x - 4) \cdot (x - 5)$

C) $f(x) = (x - 1)^2 \cdot (x + 4) \cdot (x - 5)$

D) $f(x) = (x + 1)^2 \cdot (x + 4) \cdot (x + 5)$

American Math Academy

10. Find the equation of the circle centered at $(1, -3)$ with a radius of 6.

A) $(x - 1)^2 + (y + 3)^2 = 36$

B) $(x - 1)^2 + (y + 3)^2 = 6$

C) $(x + 1)^2 + (y - 3)^2 = 36$

D) $(x + 1)^2 + (y + 3)^2 = 6$

11.
$$i^{24} + i^{36} + i^{52}$$

Which of the following is equivalent to the complex number shown above?

A) 1

B) 3

C) i

D) 3i

12. What is the value of $g(3)$ if $g(x) = \dfrac{x^2 - 3x + 5}{x + 1}$?

A) 4

B) 5

C) $\dfrac{4}{5}$

D) $\dfrac{5}{4}$

13.
$$\frac{x^{\frac{3}{2}} \cdot y^{\frac{3}{5}}}{x^{\frac{1}{2}} \cdot y^{\frac{1}{5}}}$$

Which of the following is equivalent to the expression above, where x and y are positive integers?

A) $x^{\frac{1}{2}} \cdot y^{\frac{3}{5}}$

B) $x^{\frac{1}{2}} \cdot y^{\frac{3}{5}}$

C) $x \cdot y^{\frac{2}{5}}$

D) $x^{\frac{3}{2}} \cdot y^{\frac{3}{5}}$

14. If the expression $\dfrac{1}{5}\left(x + \dfrac{k}{2}\right)\left(x - \dfrac{k}{5}\right)$, where k is a positive constant and can be rewritten as $\dfrac{1}{5}x^2 - 2$, what is the value of k?

A) 5

B) 10

C) 15

D) 25

American Math Academy

15. The total fare of five child movie tickets and one adult movie ticket costs $80. If each child's fare is one–third of each adult's ticket, what is the cost for one child ticket?

A) $10

B) $20

C) $30

D) $40

16. If $\dfrac{1}{2}x - \dfrac{2}{3}y = 20$ and $y = 15$, then find x.

17. If $a = 4\sqrt{3}$ and $5a = \sqrt{20x}$, what is the value of x?

18. If $a - b = 4$ and $a^2 - b^2 = 40$, what is the value of a?

American Math Academy

19. In the figure below, O is the center of the circle. If OB = AO = 10cm and BC = 12cm, what is the area of A(ACB)?

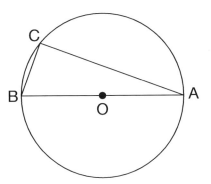

20. If $\frac{1}{2}x - ay - 8 = 0$ and the slope of the equations is $\frac{2}{7}$, then what is the value of a?

American Math Academy

PRACTICE TEST I ANSWER SHEET
NO CALCULATOR SECTION

1. Ⓐ Ⓑ Ⓒ Ⓓ
2. Ⓐ Ⓑ Ⓒ Ⓓ
3. Ⓐ Ⓑ Ⓒ Ⓓ
4. Ⓐ Ⓑ Ⓒ Ⓓ
5. Ⓐ Ⓑ Ⓒ Ⓓ

6. Ⓐ Ⓑ Ⓒ Ⓓ
7. Ⓐ Ⓑ Ⓒ Ⓓ
8. Ⓐ Ⓑ Ⓒ Ⓓ
9. Ⓐ Ⓑ Ⓒ Ⓓ
10. Ⓐ Ⓑ Ⓒ Ⓓ

11. Ⓐ Ⓑ Ⓒ Ⓓ
12. Ⓐ Ⓑ Ⓒ Ⓓ
13. Ⓐ Ⓑ Ⓒ Ⓓ
14. Ⓐ Ⓑ Ⓒ Ⓓ
15. Ⓐ Ⓑ Ⓒ Ⓓ

16.

17.

18.

19.

20.

REFERENCE SHEET

Directions

For each question from 1 to 34, solve each problem, choose the best answer from the choices provided, and fill in the corresponding bubble on your answer sheet.

- For questions 35 and 38, solve the problem and enter your answer in the grid on the answer sheet.
- Refer to the directions before question 35 for how to enter your answers in the grid. You may use any available space for scratch work.

REFERENCE

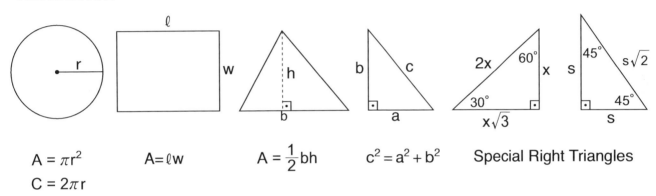

$$A = \pi r^2$$
$$C = 2\pi r$$

$$A = \ell w$$

$$A = \frac{1}{2}bh$$

$$c^2 = a^2 + b^2$$

Special Right Triangles

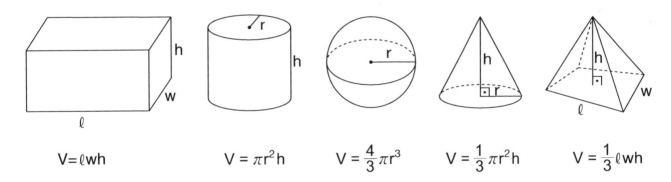

$$V = \ell w h$$

$$V = \pi r^2 h$$

$$V = \frac{4}{3}\pi r^3$$

$$V = \frac{1}{3}\pi r^2 h$$

$$V = \frac{1}{3}\ell w h$$

The number of degrees in a circle is 360.

The number of radians in a circle is 2π.

The sum of the measures in degrees of the angles of a triangle is 180.

1. Which of the following equations passes through the coordinates $(-1, 2)$ and $(3, -6)$?

   A) $y = 2x$

   B) $y = -2x$

   C) $y = 2x + 3$

   D) $y = -2x + 3$

2. $$\frac{\sqrt{yy}}{\sqrt{xx}} - \sqrt{\frac{x}{y}} - \frac{3}{2} = 0$$

   In the above equations, xx and yy are two digit numbers. Which of following could be $x \cdot y$?

   A) 9

   B) 10

   C) 12

   D) 16

3. $$x = \$7 + 11k$$
   $$y = \$15 + 7k$$

   In the equation above, x represents the price in dollars of apple juice and y represents the price in dollars of orange juice at the farmers market. K is the same amount per week. What is the price of orange juice when it's the same as the price of apple juice?

   A) $12

   B) $15

   C) $25

   D) $29

4. On the xy coordinate grid, a line K contains the points $(1, 4)$ and $(-1, 7)$. If the line L is **parallel** to line K at $(3, 1)$, which of following is the equation of the line L?

   A) $y = -\frac{3}{2}x + \frac{11}{2}$

   B) $y = \frac{3}{2}x + \frac{11}{2}$

   C) $y = -\frac{11}{2}x + \frac{3}{2}$

   D) $y = \frac{11}{2}x + \frac{3}{2}$

5. The perimeter of a rectangle is 156cm. If the width of the rectangle is three times the length, what is the width?

   A) 19.5 cm

   B) 31.5 cm

   C) 58.5 cm

   D) 60.5 cm

6. What is the value of x in the equation shown below?
   $$\frac{1}{4}(x - 5) + 8 = \frac{1}{2}x + 5$$

   A) 5

   B) 7

   C) 9

   D) 12

7. $\sqrt[4]{a\sqrt[3]{a\sqrt[2]{a}}} = \sqrt[48]{5}$. What is the value of a^{24}?

A) 5

B) 15

C) 25

D) 50

8.
$$\frac{1}{3}x + \frac{1}{4}y = 10$$
$$x - y = 2$$

In the system of equations above, solve for the y value.

A) 12

B) 16

C) 18

D) 20

9. In math team, students are trying to solve an easy test and a hard test. For each correct question in the easy test, students will earn 8 points. For each of the hard test questions, students will earn 18 points. If Jennifer solved a total of 25 questions and earned 300 points in all, how many easy questions did Jennifer solve?

A) 10

B) 15

C) 20

D) 25

10.
$$x - 2ky = 7$$
$$2x + 5y = 15$$

In the system of equations above, k is a constant. For what value of k will the system of equations have no solutions?

A) $\frac{5}{4}$

B) $-\frac{5}{4}$

C) $\frac{1}{2}$

D) $-\frac{1}{2}$

11. x and y are integer numbers.
$$-5 < x < 7$$
$$2 < y < 15$$
What is the maximum value of $x^2 - y^2$?

A) 10

B) 15

C) 20

D) 27

12. If y varies inversely as x and $x = 6$ when $y = 30$, find y when $x = 18$.

A) 5

B) 7

C) 10

D) 12

American Math Academy

13. If a, b, and c are positive numbers and $a \cdot b = \dfrac{1}{2}, b \cdot c = \dfrac{1}{4}$ and $a \cdot c = \dfrac{1}{8}$, then find $a \cdot b \cdot c$?

A) $\dfrac{1}{2}$

B) $\dfrac{1}{4}$

C) $\dfrac{1}{6}$

D) $\dfrac{1}{8}$

14. If $P(x - 2) = x^2 + 2x + 1$, then find $P(x + 1)$?

A) $x^2 + 8x + 16$

B) $-x^2 + 8x + 16$

C) $x^2 - 8x + 16$

D) $x^2 + 8x - 16$

15. There are 48 students in Science class and they are completing their classwork and then turn to their group to discuss their work. The ratio of complete work to incomplete work was 5 to 7. How many students did not complete their classwork?

A) 20

B) 22

C) 28

D) 32

16.

$$-3 < p < 2$$
$$2 < q < 5$$

From the above inequality, what is the biggest value of $p^2 + 2q$?

A) 15

B) 16

C) 17

D) 18

17. In the following figure, what is the measure of a?

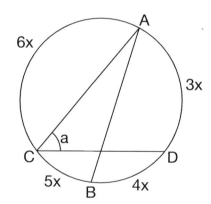

A) 15°

B) 25°

C) 30°

D) 45°

American Math Academy

18.　　　　$A = 3x+1 = 4y+2 = 5z+3$

From the above equations x, y, and z are positive integer and A is a three digit number. What is the smallest value of A?

A) 58

B) 88

C) 108

D) 128

19.　　　　$i^{2019} + i^{2020} + i^{2021}$

Which of the following is equivalent to the complex number shown above?

A) i

B) 1

C) 2i

D) 2

American Math Academy

20.

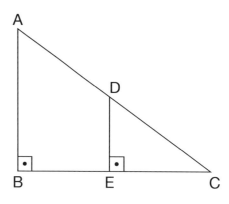

AB // DE

$|AB| = 8$

$|BC| = 6$

$|DE| = 4$, then find $|DC| + |EC|$?

A) 5

B) 6

C) 7

D) 8

21. The average of three consecutive positive integers is 54. What is the greatest possible value of one of these integers?

A) 53

B) 54

C) 55

D) 56

22. If a is the average of 2k and 2, b is the average of 4k and 8, and c is the average 6k and 20, then what is the average of a, b, and c in terms of k?

   A) k

   B) 2k

   C) 2k − 5

   D) 2k + 5

23. A letter is chosen at random from the word "mathematician." What is the probability of choosing either an A or I?

   A) $\frac{5}{13}$

   B) $\frac{4}{13}$

   C) $\frac{13}{5}$

   D) 13

24. Melisa makes an online purchase SAT book and 25% discount is applied to the book price, then 4% tax is added to this discounted price. Which of the following represents the amount Melisa pays for an item with a book price in d dollars?

   A) 0.75d

   B) 0.78d

   C) 0.88d

   D) 0.92d

25. If $f(x) - 3x = -f(x) + 2x^3$, then what is the value of f(2)?

   A) 90

   B) 10

   C) 11

   D) 12

Answer following questions 26 and 27 according to the below graph.

A car sale by years graph is given below.

Years \ Model	A	B	C
2010	20	30	10
2012	30	45	50
2014	40	90	120
2016	50	135	200
2018	100	270	320

26. Which years have the highest rate of increase for the C model?

   A) 2010 − 2012

   B) 2012 − 2014

   C) 2014 − 2016

   D) 2016 − 2018

27. What is an average sale of B model between 2010 − 2018?

A) 110

B) 114

C) 120

D) 124

Use the graph to answer questions 28 and 29.

The table below shows the number of students who attended the Science Olympiad team last year. The data is displayed in the graph.

28. What percent of the graph represents the 10th graders?

Grade	Number of Students
7th	30
8th	60
9th	90
10th	120

A) 20%

B) 30%

C) 40%

D) 50%

29. What percent of the graph represents the 9th graders?

A) 10%

B) 20%

C) 25%

D) 30%

30. If $\dfrac{x+y}{4} = \dfrac{x-c}{3}$, then find the c in terms of x and y?

A) $\dfrac{x-3y}{4}$

B) $\dfrac{x+3y}{4}$

C) $x - 3y$

D) $x + 3y$

31. Solve for x in the equation below:
$$x^2 + 4x + 5 = 0$$

A) $= 2 \pm i$

B) $= -2 \pm i$

C) $= -2 - i$

D) $= 2 + i$

American Math Academy

21

32. If $f(x) = x^2 + 2kx + c$ and the vertex point V is (1, 5), then find $k + c$.

A) 2

B) 4

C) 5

D) 8

33. Simplify $\dfrac{x^2 - 10x + 21}{x^2 - x - 6}$.

A) $\dfrac{x+7}{x+2}$

B) $\dfrac{x+7}{x-2}$

C) $\dfrac{x-7}{x-2}$

D) $\dfrac{x-7}{x+2}$

34. If $x = \dfrac{2^5}{\sqrt{8}}$, then find x.

A) $2\sqrt{2}$

B) $4\sqrt{2}$

C) $6\sqrt{2}$

D) $8\sqrt{2}$

American Math Academy

35. The population of Town A is 1.2×10^6 and the population of Town B is 24×10^3. How many times the population of Town A is greater than population of Town B?

36.

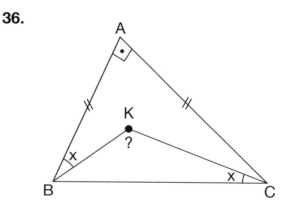

Find the angle of $\angle$ (BKC).

37. If a and b are positive integers when
$a^2 - 3b = 28$ and $b = 7$, then find a.

38. If $3x - 2y = 4$, then find $\dfrac{8^x}{4^y}$.

American Math Academy

PRACTICE TEST I ANSWER SHEET
CALCULATOR SECTION

1. (A) (B) (C) (D) 13. (A) (B) (C) (D) 24. (A) (B) (C) (D)
2. (A) (B) (C) (D) 14. (A) (B) (C) (D) 25. (A) (B) (C) (D)
3. (A) (B) (C) (D) 15. (A) (B) (C) (D) 26. (A) (B) (C) (D)
4. (A) (B) (C) (D) 16. (A) (B) (C) (D) 27. (A) (B) (C) (D)
5. (A) (B) (C) (D) 17. (A) (B) (C) (D) 28. (A) (B) (C) (D)
6. (A) (B) (C) (D) 18. (A) (B) (C) (D) 29. (A) (B) (C) (D)
7. (A) (B) (C) (D) 19. (A) (B) (C) (D) 30. (A) (B) (C) (D)
8. (A) (B) (C) (D) 20. (A) (B) (C) (D) 31. (A) (B) (C) (D)
9. (A) (B) (C) (D) 21. (A) (B) (C) (D) 32. (A) (B) (C) (D)
10. (A) (B) (C) (D) 22. (A) (B) (C) (D) 33. (A) (B) (C) (D)
11. (A) (B) (C) (D) 23. (A) (B) (C) (D) 34. (A) (B) (C) (D)
12. (A) (B) (C) (D)

35.
36.
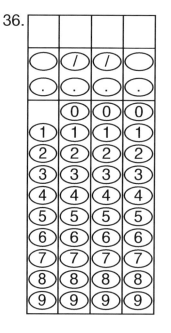
37.
38.
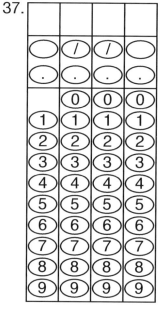

PRACTICE TEST I
NO CALCULATOR SECTION ANSWER KEY

1)	D
2)	C
3)	A
4)	C
5)	B
6)	C
7)	D
8)	D
9)	A
10)	A
11)	B
12)	D
13)	C
14)	B
15)	A
16)	60
17)	60
18)	7
19)	96 cm^2
20)	7/4

1.

$$\frac{2}{3}x + \frac{3}{4}y = 12 \qquad \qquad \frac{2}{3}x + \frac{3}{4}y = 12$$

$$-2 \cdot \left(\frac{1}{3}x + \frac{3}{2}y = 18\right) \qquad -\frac{2}{3}x - 3y = -36$$

$$\frac{3}{4}y - 3y = -24$$

$$\frac{-9y}{4} = -24$$

$$\frac{9y}{4} = 24 \ , \ y = \frac{4 \cdot 24}{9}$$

$$y = \frac{32}{3}$$

Correct Answer : D

2. $\quad x + 2y = 8$

$\quad 3x - 2y = 12$

$+$ _____

$\qquad 4x = 20$

$\qquad x = 5$

$\quad x + 2y = 8$

$\quad 5 + 2y = 8$

$\qquad 2y = 8 - 5$

$\qquad 2y = 3$

$\qquad y = \frac{3}{2}$

$\quad x + y = 5 + \frac{3}{2} = \frac{13}{2}$

Correct Answer : C

3. $\quad (x+3)^2 - 12 = (x+3) \cdot x + 3) - 12$

$$= x^2 + 3x + 3x + 9 - 12$$

$$= x^2 + 6x - 3$$

Correct Answer : A

4.

$$y = mx^2 + 3x + k$$

$$y-\text{intercept at } y = -2 \ , \ x = 0$$

$$-2 = m \cdot 0^2 + 3 \cdot 0 + k$$

$$-2 = k$$

$$x-\text{intercept at } x = 2 \ , \ y = 0$$

$$0 = m \cdot 2^2 + 3 \cdot 2 + k$$

$$0 = 4m + 6 + k$$

$$0 = 4m + 6 - 2$$

$$0 = 4m + 4$$

$$-4 = 4m$$

$$-1 = m$$

Correct Answer : C

5. $\quad \dfrac{\text{Melisa}}{2x-6} \qquad \dfrac{\text{Her sister}}{x}$

$$2x - 6 = 24$$

$$2x = 30$$

$$x = 15$$

Correct Answer : B

American Math Academy

6. $f(x) = mx^2 + k$

$f(0) = 3$

$f(0) = m \cdot 0^2 + k$

$3 = 0 + k$

$3 = k$

$f(x) = mx^2 + 3$

$f(2) = m \cdot 2^2 + 3$

$7 = 4m + 3$

$4 = 4m$

$1 = m$

$f(x) = x^2 + 3$

$f\left(-\dfrac{1}{2}\right) = \left(-\dfrac{1}{2}\right)^2 + 3$

$\qquad = \dfrac{1}{4} + 3$

$\qquad = \dfrac{13}{4}$

Correct Answer : C

7. $\left. \begin{array}{l} \sqrt{x} = 9 \ , \ x = 81 \\ y^2 = 9 \ , \ y = 3 \end{array} \right\}$ $x - y = 81 - 3 = 78$

Correct Answer : D

8.

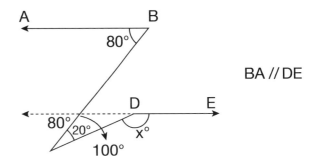

BA // DE

$x° = 100° + 20°$

$x = 120°$

Correct Answer : D

9. Since the graph has x − intercept at

x = 1, x = 4 and x = 5, then by the Factor
They are the polynomid must have factors
of (x − 1) . (x − 4) . (x − 5)

Also, the graph contains the point (2, 6).

This point satisfies the function in choice A.

Correct Answer : A

10. $(x - h)^2 + (y - k)^2 = r^2$

$(x - 1)^2 + (y + 3)^2 = 36$

Correct Answer : A

American Math Academy

11. $i^{24} + i^{36} + i^{52}$

$\boxed{\text{Rule}: i^2 = -1}$

$= (i^2)^{12} + (i^2)^{18} + (i^2)^{26}$

$= (-1)^{12} + (-1)^{18} + (-1)^{26}$

$= 1 + 1 + 1$

$= 3$

Correct Answer : B

12. $g(x) = \dfrac{x^2 - 3x + 5}{x + 1}$

$g(3) = \dfrac{3^2 - 3 \cdot 3 + 5}{3 + 1}$

$= \dfrac{9 - 9 + 5}{4}$

$= \dfrac{5}{4}$

Correct Answer : D

13. $\dfrac{x^{\frac{3}{2}} \cdot y^{\frac{3}{5}}}{x^{\frac{1}{2}} \cdot x^{\frac{1}{5}}} = x^{\frac{3}{2} - \frac{1}{2}} \cdot y^{\frac{3}{5} - \frac{1}{5}}$

$= x^{\frac{2}{2}} \cdot y^{\frac{2}{5}}$

$= x \cdot y^{\frac{2}{5}}$

Correct Answer : C

14. $\dfrac{1}{5}\left(x + \dfrac{k}{2}\right) \cdot \left(x - \dfrac{k}{5}\right) = \dfrac{1}{5}x^2 - 2$

$\dfrac{1}{5}\left(x^2 - \dfrac{k^2}{10}\right) = \dfrac{1}{5}x^2 - 2$

$\dfrac{1}{5}x^2 - \dfrac{k^2}{50} = \dfrac{1}{5}x^2 - 2$

$\dfrac{-k^2}{50} = -2$

$k^2 = 100 \ , \ k = \mp 10$

$k = 10 \,(\text{since } k \text{ is positive integers})$

Correct Answer : B

15. Child ticket + Adult ticket = Total Fare

$5C + A = \$80$

If each child's ticket is $\dfrac{1}{3}$ of adult ticket

$C = \dfrac{1}{3}A \ , \ A = 3C$

$5C + A = \$80$

$5C + 3C = \$80 \qquad 8C = \$80$

$\qquad\qquad\qquad\qquad C = \$10$

Correct Answer : A

16. $\dfrac{1}{2}x - \dfrac{2}{3}y = 20 \ , \ y = 15$

$\dfrac{1}{2}x - \dfrac{2}{3}(15) = 20$

$\dfrac{1}{2}x - \dfrac{30}{3} = 20$

$\dfrac{1}{2}x - 10 = 20$

$\dfrac{1}{2}x = 30$

$x = 60$

Correct Answer : 60

American Math Academy

17. $a = 4\sqrt{3}$ and $5a = \sqrt{20x}$

$5(4\sqrt{3}) = \sqrt{20x}$

$(20\sqrt{3})^2 = (\sqrt{20x})^2$

$400 \cdot 3 = 20x$

$\dfrac{1200}{20} = x$

$60 = x$

Correct Answer : 60

19.

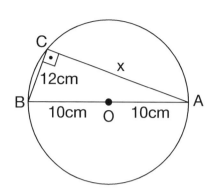

Use pythagorean theorem for right triangle.

$(12cm)^2 + x^2 = (20cm)^2$

$144cm^2 + x^2 = 400cm^2$

$x^2 = 400cm^2 - 144cm^2$

$x^2 = 256cm^2$

$x = 16cm$

Area of $A(ACB) = \dfrac{12cm \cdot 16cm}{2} = 96cm^2$

Correct Answer : 96cm²

18. $a - b = 4$ and $a^2 - b^2 = 40$

$(a - b) \cdot (a + b) = 40$

$4(a + b) = 40$

$a + b = 10$

$a - b = 4$

$+\quad a + b = 10$

―――――――――

$2a = 14$ $a = 7$

Correct Answer : 7

20. $\dfrac{1}{2}x - ay = 8$

slope intercept form $y = mx + b$

$\dfrac{1}{2}x - 8 = ay$

$\dfrac{1}{2a}x - \dfrac{8}{a} = y$ slope $= \dfrac{1}{2a}$

$\dfrac{1}{2a} = \dfrac{2}{7}$, $4a = 7$

$a = \dfrac{7}{4}$

Correct Answer : $\dfrac{7}{4}$

American Math Academy

PRACTICE TEST I
CALCULATOR SECTION ANSWER KEY

1)	B		20)	D
2)	D		21)	C
3)	D		22)	D
4)	A		23)	A
5)	C		24)	B
6)	B		25)	C
7)	C		26)	A
8)	B		27)	B
9)	B		28)	C
10)	B		29)	D
11)	D		30)	A
12)	C		31)	B
13)	D		32)	C
14)	A		33)	D
15)	C		34)	D
16)	D		35)	50
17)	C		36)	135°
18)	A		37)	7
19)	B		38)	16

1. The slope of points $(-1, -2)$ and $(3, -6)$.

$$m = \frac{y_2 - y_1}{x_2 - x_1}$$

$$m = \frac{-6 - (2)}{3 - (-1)} = \frac{-8}{4} = -2$$

Slope - intercept form

$y = mx + b$

$y = -2x + b$,(use one of the above points to find b constant)

$-6 = -2(3) + b$

$-6 = -6 + b$

$-6 + 6 = b$

$\quad 0 = b$

$\quad y = -2x$

Correct Answer : B

2. $\sqrt{\dfrac{11y}{11x}} - \sqrt{\dfrac{x}{y}} - \dfrac{3}{2} = 0$

$\dfrac{\sqrt{y}}{\sqrt{x}} - \dfrac{\sqrt{x}}{\sqrt{y}} = \dfrac{3}{2}$ (Find common denominator)

$\dfrac{\sqrt{y} \cdot (\sqrt{y})}{\sqrt{x} \cdot (\sqrt{y})} - \dfrac{\sqrt{x} \cdot (\sqrt{x})}{\sqrt{y} \cdot (\sqrt{x})} = \dfrac{3}{2}$

$\dfrac{\sqrt{y^2}}{\sqrt{xy}} - \dfrac{\sqrt{x^2}}{\sqrt{xy}} = \dfrac{3}{2}$

$\dfrac{y}{\sqrt{xy}} - \dfrac{x}{\sqrt{xy}} = \dfrac{3}{2}$

$\dfrac{y - x}{\sqrt{xy}} = \dfrac{3}{2}$, then x could be 8 and y could be 2.

$x \cdot y = 2 \cdot 8 = 16$

Correct Answer : D

3. $x = \$7 + 11k \longrightarrow$ price of apple juice

$y = \$15 + 7k \longrightarrow$ price of orange juice

$x = y$ because price of orange juice is the same as the price of apple juice.

$\$7 + 11k = \$15 + 7k$

$11k - 7k = \$15 - \$7$

$4k = \$8$

$k = \$2$

$y = \$15 + 7k \longrightarrow$ price of orange juice

$y = \$15 + 7(\$2)$

$y = \$15 + \$14$

$y = \$29$

Correct Answer : D

4. Line K contains the points $(1, 4)$ and $(-1, 7)$.

Slope of point K

$$m = \frac{y_2 - y_1}{x_2 - x_1} = \frac{7 - 4}{-1 - (1)} = \frac{3}{-2} = -\frac{3}{2}$$

Since line K is parallel to line L slopes are same.

Slope of point L is $-\dfrac{3}{2}$.

Slope - intercept form

$y = mx + b$

$y = -\dfrac{3}{2} x + b$ (use one of the above points to find b constant)

$7 = -\dfrac{3}{2} (-1) + b$

$7 = \dfrac{3}{2} + b$

$7 - \dfrac{3}{2} = b$

$\dfrac{11}{2} = b$

Equation of line L $\longrightarrow y = -\dfrac{3}{2} + \dfrac{11}{2}$

Correct Answer : A

5. The perimeter of the rectangular is 156cm.

$2L + 2W = 156cm$

$W = 3L$

$2L + 2(3L) = 156cm$

$2L + 6L = 156cm$

$8L = 156cm$

$L = 19.5cm$

$W = 58.5cm$

Correct Answer : C

6. $\frac{1}{4}(x-5)+8 = \frac{1}{2}x+5$

$4 \cdot \left[\frac{1}{4}(x-5)+8 = \frac{1}{2}x+5\right]$

(Multiply both sides of the equation of equation with common factors to take out denominators)

$\frac{4x}{4} - \frac{20}{4} + 32 = \frac{4x}{2} + 20$

$x - 5 + 32 = 2x + 20$

$x + 27 = 2x + 20$

$27 - 20 = 2x - x$, $x = 7$

Correct Answer : B

7. $\sqrt[4.3.4]{(a^3)^2 \cdot a^2 \cdot a^4} = \sqrt[48]{a^6 \cdot a^2 \cdot a^4} = \sqrt[48]{a^{12}}$

$\sqrt[48]{a^{12}} = \sqrt[48]{5}$

$a^{12} = 5$, then $a^{24} = 5^2 = 25$

Correct Answer : C

8. $\frac{1}{3}x + \frac{1}{4}y = 10$

(Multiply both side of equation with common factors to take out denominators)

$12\left[\frac{1}{3}x + \frac{1}{4}y = 10\right] = 4x + 3y = 120$

$\begin{pmatrix} 4x + 3y = 120 \\ 3(x - y = 2) \end{pmatrix}$ Use elimination method to find x and y.

$(4x + 3y = 120)$

$+ \quad \underline{(3x - 3y = 6)}$

$7x = 126$

$x = 18$

$y = 16$

Correct Answer : B

9. Easy questions: e

Hard questions: h

$\begin{pmatrix} e + h = 25 \\ 8e + 18h = 2 \end{pmatrix}$ Use elimination method to find e and h.

$\begin{matrix} -8(e + h = 25) \\ 8e + 18h = 300 \end{matrix} = \begin{matrix} -8e - 8h = -200 \\ 8e + 18h = 300 \end{matrix}$

$10h = 100$, then $h = 10$ and $e = 15$.

Correct Answer : B

American Math Academy

10. If the systems of equations have no soluti-ons that mean equations have same slope.

$$x - 2ky = 7$$
$$2x + 5y = 15$$

NOTE: slope is a number next to the x−axis over a number next to the y−axis and sing is always opposite.

Slope of 1st equation is : $\dfrac{1}{2k}$

Slope of 2nd equation is : $-\dfrac{2}{5}$

Since slopes are equal.

$$\dfrac{1}{2k} = -\dfrac{2}{5}$$

$$-4k = 5$$

$$k = -\dfrac{5}{4}$$

Correct Answer : B

11. $\left.\begin{array}{l} -5 < x < 7 \\ 2 < y < 15 \end{array}\right\}$ since x and y are integers, x maximum can be 6 and y mi-nimum can be 3.

$$x^2 - y^2 = 6^2 - 3^2$$
$$= 36 - 9$$
$$= 27$$

Correct Answer : D

12. $y = \dfrac{k}{x}$ (inverse variation)

If x = 6 when y = 30, then $30 = \dfrac{k}{6}$ and k = 180.

Use the same formula to find y when x = 18.

$y = \dfrac{k}{x} \longrightarrow y = \dfrac{180}{18}$, then y=10

Correct Answer : C

---

13. $a \cdot b = \dfrac{1}{2}$

$b \cdot c = \dfrac{1}{4}$

$a \cdot c = \dfrac{1}{8}$

Let multiply all together;

$$a^2 \cdot b^2 \cdot c^2 = \dfrac{1}{2} \cdot \dfrac{1}{4} \cdot \dfrac{1}{8}$$

$$a^2 \cdot b^2 \cdot c^2 = \dfrac{1}{64}$$

$$\sqrt{a^2 \cdot b^2 \cdot c^2} = \sqrt{\dfrac{1}{64}}$$

$a \cdot b \cdot c = \pm\dfrac{1}{8}$, Since a, b, and c are positive numbers

$a \cdot b \cdot c = \dfrac{1}{8}$

Correct Answer : D

14. $P(x - 2) = x^2 + 2x + 1$

To find P (x + 1) plug in x + 3 for x in P(x − 2).

$P(x + 3 - 2) = (x + 3)^2 + 2(x + 3) + 1$

$P(x + 1) = x^2 + 6x + 9 + 2x + 6 + 1$

$P(x + 1) = x^2 + 8x + 16$

Correct Answer : A

American Math Academy

15. Ratio of complete work to incomplete work is 5 to 7.

$$5x + 7x = 48$$
$$12x = 48$$
$$x = 4$$

Complete work: $5x = 5 \cdot 4 = 20$

Incomplete work: $7x = 7 \cdot 4 = 28$

Correct Answer : C

16.

$$p^2 \longrightarrow 4 < p^2 < 9$$
$$2q \longrightarrow 4 < 2q < 10$$
$$+$$
$$\overline{\quad\quad\quad\quad\quad\quad}$$
$$8 < p^2 + 2q < 19$$

Highest value of $p^2 + 2q$ is 18.

Correct Answer : D

17.

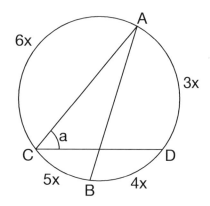

$$6x + 5x + 4x + 3x = 360°$$
$$18x = 360°$$
$$x = 20 \quad , \quad 2a = 3x$$
$$2a = 60° \quad , \quad a = 30°$$

Correct Answer : C

18. If $A = 3x + 1 = 4y + 2 = 5z + 3$,

then $A + 2 = 3x + 3 = 4y + 4 = 5z + 5$.

$A + 2 = 3(x + 1) = 4(y + 1) = 5(z + 1)$

$A + 2 = $ LCM $(3, 4, 5) = 60$.

$A + 2 = 60$, then $A = 58$

Correct Answer : A

19. $\boxed{i^2 = -1}$

$$(i^2)^{1009} \cdot i + (i^2)^{1010} + (i^2)^{1010} \cdot i$$
$$(-1)^{1009} \cdot i + (-1)^{2010} + (-1)^{1010} \cdot i$$
$$= -i + 1 + i$$
$$= 1$$

Correct Answer : B

American Math Academy

20.

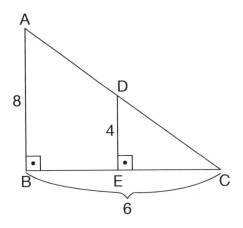

$|AC| = 6^2 + 8^2 = 10^2$

$|AC| = 10$

$\dfrac{4}{8} = \dfrac{|DC|}{|AC|}$, $\dfrac{1}{2} = \dfrac{|DC|}{10}$

$|DC| = 5$

$\dfrac{1}{2} = \dfrac{|EC|}{|BC|}$, $\dfrac{1}{2} = \dfrac{|EC|}{6}$

$|EC| = 3$

$|DC| + |EC| = 5 + 3 = 8$

Correct Answer : D

21.

$$\dfrac{x + x + 1 + x + 2}{3} = 54$$

$\dfrac{3x + 3}{3} = 54$

$3x + 3 = 162$

$3x = 162 - 3$

$3x = 159$

$x = 53$

Greatest possible one x + 2 = 53 + 2 = 55

Correct Answer : C

22. $a = \dfrac{2k + 2}{2} = k + 1$

$b = \dfrac{4k + 8}{2} = 2k + 4$

$c = \dfrac{6k + 20}{2} = 3k + 10$

Average of a, b and c

$\dfrac{a + b + c}{3} = \dfrac{k + 1 + 2k + 4 + 3k + 10}{3}$

$= \dfrac{6k + 15}{3} = 2k + 5$

Correct Answer : D

23. Probability of A or I

total A = 3

total I = 2

$\dfrac{\text{total A and I}}{\text{total letters}} = \dfrac{5}{13}$

Correct Answer : A

24. If d represents the price of the book, then
d − 0.25 d = 0.75d (the price of book after
the discount)

If a 4% tax is added, the final price 0.75d +
0.04(0.75 d) = 0.78d

Correct Answer : B

25. $f(x) + f(x) = 2x^3 + 3x$

$f(x) + f(x) = 2x^3 + 3x$

$2f(x) = 2x^3 + 3x$

$f(x) = \dfrac{2x^3 + 3x}{2}$

$f(2) = \dfrac{2 \cdot 2^3 + 3 \cdot 2}{2} = 11$

Correct Answer : C

26. Between $2010 - 2012$,

$2010 \longrightarrow 10$ sales

$2012 \longrightarrow 50$ sales

40 increase.

If 10 sales $\longrightarrow 40$ increase

100 sales $\longrightarrow$ x increase

$x = 400\%$ is the highest increased .

Correct Answer : A

27. Total sale of B model between

$2010 - 2018 : 30 + 45 + 90 + 135 + 270$

$= 570$ car.

Total years : 5 years

Average: $\dfrac{570}{5} = 114$ car.

Correct Answer : B

28. Total # of students

$= 120 + 90 + 60 + 30 + 300$ students.

Total 10th grade $= 120$ students.

Average of 10th grade students

$= \dfrac{120}{300} = \dfrac{2}{5} = 40\%$

Correct Answer : C

29. Total # of students

$= 120 + 90 + 60 + 30 = 300$

Total 9th graders $= 90$ students.

Average of 9th graders

$= \dfrac{90}{300} = \dfrac{3}{10} = 30\%$

Correct Answer : D

30. $\dfrac{x + y}{4} = \dfrac{x - c}{3} \longrightarrow$ (Cross multiply)

$4(x - c) = 3(x + y)$ (use distributive property)

$4x - 4c = 3x + 3y$

$4x - 3x - 3y = 4c$

$x - 3y = 4c$ (divided by 4 each term to find c)

$\dfrac{x}{4} - \dfrac{3y}{4} = c$

$\dfrac{x - 3y}{4} = c$

Correct Answer : A

31. $x^2 + 4x + 5 = 0$ (Use the complete square method to solve equation)

$x^2 + 4x = -5$

$(x + 2)^2 - 4 = -5$

$(x + 2)^2 = -5 + 4$

$(x + 2)^2 = -1 \qquad i^2 = -1$

$x + 2 = \pm i$

$x = -2 \pm i$

Correct Answer : B

32. $f(x) = x^2 + 2kx + c$

$x = \dfrac{-b}{2a}$ (Axis of symmetry)

$x = \dfrac{-b}{2a}$

$x = \dfrac{-2k}{2}$

$1 = \dfrac{-2k}{2}$ (since $x = 1$)

$2 = -2k$

$-1 = k$

$V(1, 5) \longrightarrow$ plug this point in to the equation

$5 = 1^2 + 2k(1) + c$

$4 = 2k + c \quad , \quad k = -1$

$4 = 2(-1) + c$

$4 + 2 = c$

$6 = c$

$k + c = 6 + (-1) = 5$

Correct Answer : C

33. $\dfrac{x^2 - 10x + 21}{x^2 - x - 6} = \dfrac{(x - 7)(x\cancel{-3})}{(x + 2)(x\cancel{-3})} \longrightarrow$ (simplify)

$\dfrac{x - 7}{x + 2}$

Correct Answer : D

34. $x = \dfrac{2^5}{\sqrt{8}},$

$x = \dfrac{32}{2\sqrt{2}}$ (simplify)

$x = \dfrac{16}{\sqrt{2}}$ (multiply by $\sqrt{2}$ part and whole)

$x = \dfrac{16}{\sqrt{2}} \cdot \dfrac{\sqrt{2}}{\sqrt{2}}$

$x = \dfrac{16\sqrt{2}}{2}$

$x = 8\sqrt{2}$

Correct Answer : D

35. Town A is 1.2×10^6

Town B is 24×10^3

$\dfrac{\text{population of Town A}}{\text{population of Town B}} = \dfrac{1.2 \times 10^6}{24 \times 10^3}$

$\dfrac{12 \times 10^5}{24 \times 10^3} = \dfrac{1 \times 10^5}{2 \times 10^3} = \dfrac{1}{2} \cdot 10^{5-3}$

$= \dfrac{1}{2} \cdot 10^2$

$= 50$

Correct Answer : 50

American Math Academy

36.

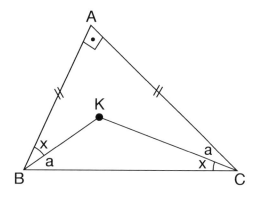

$2x + 2a + 90° = 180°$

$x + a = 45°$

$< (BCK) + x + a = 180°$

$< (BCK) + 45° = 180°$

$< (BCK) = 135°$

Correct Answer : 135°

37. $a^2 - 3b = 28$ and $b = 7$

$a^2 - 3(7) = 28$

$a^2 - 21 = 28$

$a^2 = 28 + 21$

$a^2 = 49$

$a = \pm 7$ (since a is positive integer a can be only 7)

$a = 7$

Correct Answer : 7

38. $3x - 3y = 4$

$$\frac{8^x}{4^y} = \frac{2^{3x}}{2^{2y}} = 2^{3x - 2y} = 2^4 = 16$$

Correct Answer : 16

REFERENCE SHEET

Directions

For each question from 1 to 15, solve each problem, choose the best answer from the choices provided, and fill in the corresponding bubble on your answer sheet.

- For questions 16 to 20, solve the problem and enter your answer in the grid on the answer sheet.
- Refer to the directions before question 18 for how to enter your answers in the grid. You may use any available space for scratch work.

REFERENCE

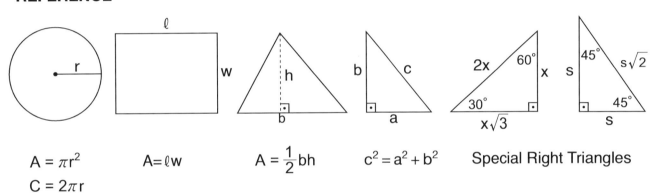

$A = \pi r^2$

$C = 2\pi r$

$A = \ell w$

$A = \frac{1}{2}bh$

$c^2 = a^2 + b^2$

Special Right Triangles

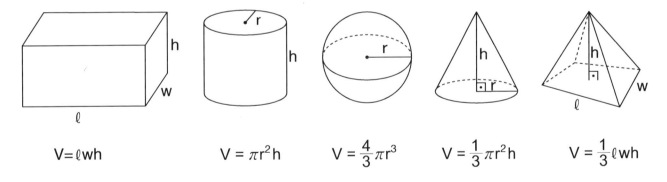

$V = \ell wh$

$V = \pi r^2 h$

$V = \frac{4}{3}\pi r^3$

$V = \frac{1}{3}\pi r^2 h$

$V = \frac{1}{3}\ell wh$

The number of degrees in a circle is 360.

The number of radians in a circle is 2π.

The sum of the measures in degrees of the angles of a triangle is 180.

1. Which of the following is equivalent to $\left(x+\dfrac{x}{2}\right)^2$?

A) $\dfrac{x^2}{4}$

B) $\dfrac{9x^2}{4}$

C) $\dfrac{4x^2}{9}$

D) $\dfrac{5x^2}{4}$

2. The height of a trunk is between $\sqrt{2}$ meters and $\sqrt{8}$ meters. Which of the following could be the height of the trunk?

A) $\dfrac{1}{65}$

B) $\dfrac{5}{2}$

C) $\dfrac{37}{8}$

D) $\dfrac{11}{3}$

3. How many liters of 80% pure water must be added to 40 liters of a 30% pure water to produce 60% pure water?

A) 30 liters

B) 40 liters

C) 50 liters

D) 60 liters

4.
$$2a + 3b = 18$$
$$3b - 5a = 11$$
What is the value of $a - b$?

A) 3

B) 13

C) $\dfrac{-13}{3}$

D) $\dfrac{13}{3}$

5. The population of a city is increased from 120,000 to 168,000. Find the percentage of the increase.

A) 20%

B) 30%

C) 40%

D) 50%

6. What is the solution to the equation below?
$$\frac{2}{x-3} = \frac{5}{2x-7}$$

A) 1

B) −1

C) 2

D) −2

American Math Academy

7. If $x^3 = 64$, then find x^2.

A) 2

B) 4

C) 8

D) 16

8. Henry went to the supermarket. He needed to buy 8 eggs and 4 liter of milk. 1 egg cost \$2 and 1 liter of milk cost $\$2^2$. At the end of shopping trip he paid $\$2^a$. Find the value of a.

A) 3

B) 4

C) 5

D) 6

9. What is the solution of the equation given below?

$$\frac{\sqrt{2} \cdot 6^{\frac{1}{3}}}{\sqrt[3]{3} \cdot 2^{-\frac{1}{6}}}$$

A) 1

B) 2

C) 3

D) 4

10. Tom has a garden, which is 24 feet in height and 32 feet in width. He wants to plant trees around his garden. The price of a tree is \$5. At least how much does he have to pay for the trees?

A) \$50

B) \$60

C) \$70

D) \$80

11. The sum of the three consecutive even numbers is 42. What is half of the smallest number?

A) 4

B) 6

C) 8

D) 10

American Math Academy

12.

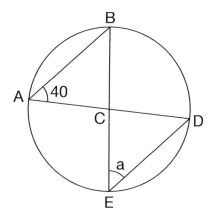

If C is the center of the circle then find the arc AE.

A) 60°

B) 80°

C) 100°

D) 120°

13. Which of the following is equal to $\dfrac{x^2}{9} - \dfrac{y^2}{4}$?

A) $\left(\dfrac{x}{3} - \dfrac{y}{2}\right) \cdot \left(\dfrac{x}{3} - \dfrac{y}{2}\right)$

B) $\left(\dfrac{x}{3} + \dfrac{y}{2}\right) \cdot \left(\dfrac{x}{3} - \dfrac{y}{2}\right)$

C) $\left(\dfrac{x}{3} + \dfrac{y}{2}\right) \cdot \left(\dfrac{x}{3} + \dfrac{y}{2}\right)$

D) $\left(\dfrac{x}{2} - \dfrac{y}{3}\right) \cdot \left(\dfrac{x}{2} + \dfrac{y}{3}\right)$

14.
$$\frac{3(x+5)-8}{7} = \frac{17-(6-x)}{5}$$

In the equation above, what is the value of x?

A) $\dfrac{21}{4}$

B) $\dfrac{11}{4}$

C) $\dfrac{4}{21}$

D) $\dfrac{23}{4}$

15. Which of the following complex numbers are equivalent to $\left(\dfrac{1+i}{1-i}\right)^{2018?}$

A) 1

B) −1

C) i

D) −i

American Math Academy

16.

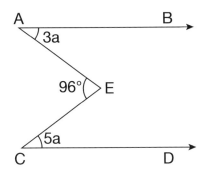

In the figure above, AB is parallel to CD. What is the angle of $\angle(BAE)$?

17. What is the average test score for the class if 6 students received scores of: 88, 85, 95, 66, 75 and 80?

18. In the polynomial below c is the constant. If the polynomial f(x) is divisible by x−4 then find the value of c.

$$f(x) = x^2 - 2cx + 8$$

19. If $x = 1- \sqrt{3}$ and $y = 1 + \sqrt{3}$ then find $x \cdot y$?

20. Simplify $\sqrt[4]{0.0016}$

American Math Academy

43

PRACTICE TEST II ANSWER SHEET
NO CALCULATOR SECTION

1. Ⓐ Ⓑ Ⓒ Ⓓ   6. Ⓐ Ⓑ Ⓒ Ⓓ   11. Ⓐ Ⓑ Ⓒ Ⓓ

2. Ⓐ Ⓑ Ⓒ Ⓓ   7. Ⓐ Ⓑ Ⓒ Ⓓ   12. Ⓐ Ⓑ Ⓒ Ⓓ

3. Ⓐ Ⓑ Ⓒ Ⓓ   8. Ⓐ Ⓑ Ⓒ Ⓓ   13. Ⓐ Ⓑ Ⓒ Ⓓ

4. Ⓐ Ⓑ Ⓒ Ⓓ   9. Ⓐ Ⓑ Ⓒ Ⓓ   14. Ⓐ Ⓑ Ⓒ Ⓓ

5. Ⓐ Ⓑ Ⓒ Ⓓ   10. Ⓐ Ⓑ Ⓒ Ⓓ   15. Ⓐ Ⓑ Ⓒ Ⓓ

16.

17.

18.

19.

20.

REFERENCE SHEET

Directions

For each question from 1 to 34, solve each problem, choose the best answer from the choices provided, and fill in the corresponding bubble on your answer sheet.

- For questions 35 and 38, solve the problem and enter your answer in the grid on the answer sheet.

- Refer to the directions before question 35 for how to enter your answers in the grid. You may use any available space for scratch work.

REFERENCE

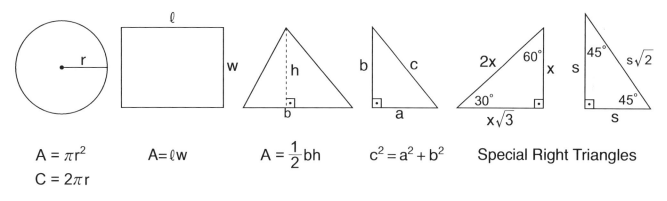

$A = \pi r^2$ $A = \ell w$ $A = \frac{1}{2} bh$ $c^2 = a^2 + b^2$ Special Right Triangles

$C = 2\pi r$

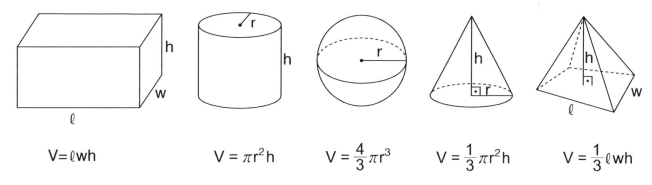

$V = \ell wh$ $V = \pi r^2 h$ $V = \frac{4}{3}\pi r^3$ $V = \frac{1}{3}\pi r^2 h$ $V = \frac{1}{3}\ell wh$

The number of degrees in a circle is 360.

The number of radians in a circle is 2π.

The sum of the measures in degrees of the angles of a triangle is 180.

1. What is the solution of the equation given below?

$$\frac{\sqrt{3}\cdot\sqrt[3]{27}}{\sqrt[3]{8}\cdot\sqrt{2}}?$$

A) $\dfrac{3\sqrt{2}}{4}$

B) $\dfrac{2\sqrt{2}}{3}$

C) $\sqrt{2}$

D) $\sqrt{3}$

2. Let A and B be two sets.

$A = \{-7, -6, -5, -4, -3, -2, -1, 0, 1, 2, 3, 4, 5, 6\}$

$B = \{-9, -7, -5, -3, -1, 3, 5, 7, 9\}$

Which of the following is the given set of $s(A \cap B)$?

A) $(-9, -5, -3, -1, 0, 1, 3, 5)$

B) $(-7, -5, -3, -1, 3, 5)$

C) $(-9, -7, -5, -3, -1, 3, 5, 6)$

D) $(-7, -5, -3, -1, 1, 2, 3, 4, 5)$

3. In a college there will be an election for the head of students. There are three candidates: Mike, Julia, and Peter. Mike has 30% of the votes, Julia has 60% of votes, and Peter has 10% of votes. In the election 500 votes were collected. What is difference between Julia and Mike?

A) 50

B) 150

C) 200

D) 250

4. $f(x) = 3x - 6$. What is the solution of $f(2) + f^{-1}(3)$?

A) 1

B) 2

C) 3

D) 4

5. $A\{0, 1, 2, 3, 4, 5, 6, 7, 8, 9\}$

What is the probability of the selecting an odd number in the set A?

A) $\dfrac{1}{2}$

B) $\dfrac{1}{3}$

C) $\dfrac{1}{4}$

D) $\dfrac{1}{5}$

American Math Academy

6.

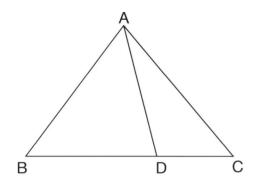

If $|AD| = |BD|$

$m(\widehat{ABD}) = 70$

$m(\widehat{BCA}) = 30$

What is the angle of $\angle(DAC)$?

A) $3°$

B) $5°$

C) $10°$

D) $15°$

8.

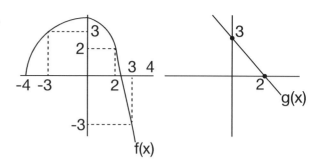

f and g are two functions and their graph is given above.

What is the solution of $f(g(4)) + f(3)$?

A) -2

B) -1

C) 0

D) 1

7.

$$\triangle = x^2 - 2x + 1$$
$$\bigcirc = x^2 - 1$$

From the above if $\bigcirc = \triangle$, then find x.

A) 1

B) 2

C) 3

D) 4

9. Find $\cos30° \cdot \sin60° \cdot \tan60°$?

A) $\dfrac{\sqrt{3}}{3}$

B) $\dfrac{3}{4}$

C) $\sqrt{3}$

D) $\dfrac{3\sqrt{3}}{4}$

American Math Academy

10.

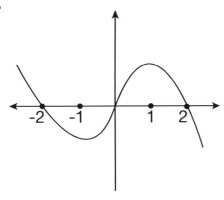

Which of the following could be the equation of the graph above?

A) $x(x - 2)(x + 2)$

B) $x(x - 2)^2$

C) $x(x + 2)^2$

D) $(x - 2)(x + 2)$

11.

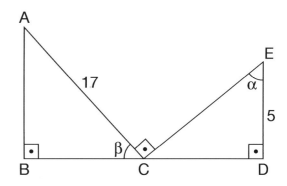

If AB $\perp$ BC

ED $\perp$ CD

AC $\perp$ CE

$|BD| = 27$

$|AB| = 8$

$|AC| = 17$

$|ED| = 5$

From the above triangles, find Sin α · Cot β?

A) $\dfrac{29}{45}$

B) $\dfrac{45}{29}$

C) $\dfrac{26}{45}$

D) $\dfrac{45}{26}$

American Math Academy

48

12.

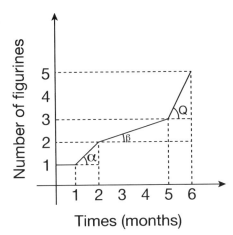

On what interval did the number of figurines decrease the fastest?

A) Between 1 and 2 months

B) Between 2 and 5 months

C) Between 1 and 1 months

D) Between 5 and 6 months

13.

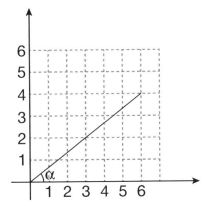

What is the equation of the function?

A) $y = 2x$

B) $y = \dfrac{2}{3}x$

C) $y = x + 7$

D) $y = 2x + 3$

14. The width of the rectangular dance floor is $x + 8$ feet. The length of the floor is 3 feet longer than it is wide. Which of the following expresses the perimeter, in feet, of the dance floor in terms area of x?

A) $3x^2 + 7$

B) $8x^2 + 23x + 16$

C) $x^2 + 19x + 88$

D) $x^2 + 23x + 17$

15. $$ax^3 + bx^2 + cx + d = 0$$

In the equation above, a,b,c and d are constants. If the equation roots are $-2, 4$ and -7, which of the following is a factor of $ax^3 + bx^2 + cx + d$?

A) $x - 2$

B) $x + 4$

C) $x + 7$

D) $x - 7$

16. $$f(x) = (x-4)^2 + 11$$
$$g(x) = 2x + 2.$$

What is one possible value of $f(a) = g(a)$?

A) 1

B) 2

C) 3

D) 5

17. $[\{(a+b) \div c\} \cdot d] - e = 3$

In the above equations, if $a = 12$, $b = 18$, $c = 10$ and $d = 3$, then find the value of e.

A) 3

B) 6

C) 9

D) 12

Use the following graph to answer questions 18 and 19.

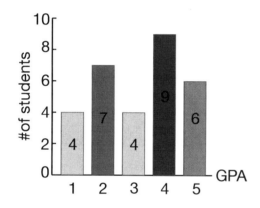

The graph given above is about the number of students and their GPA.

18. What percent of students have a GPA of 5.0?

A) 15

B) 20

C) 25

D) 30

19. What is the average GPA (Grade Point Average) for all of the students?

A) 2.8

B) 3.0

C) 3.2

D) 3.5

20. Solve $(\tan\alpha \cdot \cos\alpha)^2 + (\sin\alpha \cdot \cot\alpha)^2$?

A) $\sin\alpha$

B) $\cos\alpha$

C) 1

D) $\tan\alpha$

21. What is the sum of the solutions for $x^2 + x - 12 = 0$?

A) −2

B) −1

C) 1

D) 2

American Math Academy

22.
$$2a - 3b = 12$$
$$3a + 5b = 18$$

For the solution (a, b) to the system of equations above, what is the value of $a - b$?

A) 2

B) 4

C) 6

D) 8

23. $\dfrac{1}{a} = \dfrac{1}{b} + \dfrac{1}{c}$ Find b in terms of a and c.

A) $b = \dfrac{ac}{c-a}$

B) $b = \dfrac{ac}{a-c}$

C) $b = ac$

D) $b = \dfrac{1}{c-a}$

24. Solve for x in the equation below:
$$x^2 + 4x - 8 = 0$$

A) $x = -2 \pm 2\sqrt{3}$

B) $x = 2 \pm 2\sqrt{3}$

C) $x = 2 + \sqrt{3}$

D) $x = 2 - \sqrt{3}$

Use the following chart to answer questions 25 to 27

	With glasses	No glasses
Girl	10	6
Boy	6	12

The chart is about the students in the class and their situation with glasses.

American Math Academy

25. What is the probability of the selected student has no glasses?

A) $\dfrac{8}{17}$

B) $\dfrac{9}{17}$

C) $\dfrac{10}{17}$

D) $\dfrac{21}{34}$

26. What is the probability of the selected student is a girl?

A) $\dfrac{8}{17}$

B) $\dfrac{9}{17}$

C) $\dfrac{11}{17}$

D) $\dfrac{12}{17}$

27. What is the probability of the selected student is no glasses and girls?

A) $\dfrac{1}{17}$

B) $\dfrac{2}{17}$

C) $\dfrac{3}{17}$

D) $\dfrac{4}{17}$

28. Which of the following tables does not represent linear relations?

A)
X	Y
1	0
2	2
3	4
4	6

B)
X	Y
−1	−3
−2	−6
−3	−9
−4	−12

C)
X	Y
2	6
4	12
6	18
8	24

D)
X	Y
1	2
3	0
5	3
1	6

29. If a ratio of $\dfrac{1}{3} : \dfrac{1}{b}$ is equal to $\dfrac{1}{18} : \dfrac{1}{12}$ what is the value of b?

A) 9

B) $\dfrac{9}{2}$

C) $\dfrac{2}{9}$

D) 2

30. If $x^2 + ax - 10 = (x - 1)(bx + c)$ then find a + c.

A) 9

B) 19

C) 18

D) 21

31. If $3^{2x-16} = 27^{x-6}$, then what is the value of x?

A) 1

B) −1

C) −2

D) 2

32. If $x > 0$ and $x - 3 = \sqrt{x-3}$ then which of following can be x?

A) 0

B) 1

C) 2

D) 4

33. Which of the following graph shows direct variation?

A)

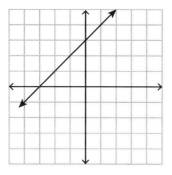

B)

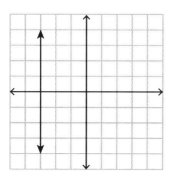

C)

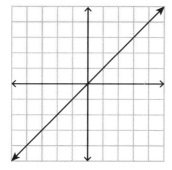

D)

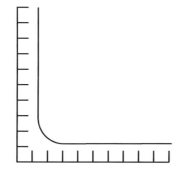

American Math Academy

34. Which of the following is equal to $\dfrac{81^2 \cdot 9^3}{3^{10}}$?

A) 3^7

B) 3^4

C) 3^3

D) 3^0

35. The following table shows 2019 salaries for four soccer players. What is the difference from highest salary to lowest salary?

Player A	3.41×10^8
Player B	2.20×10^7
Player C	2.23×10^7
Player D	3.23×10^8

36. Two numbers have a ratio of 5 to 2. If they are positive numbers and differ by 15, what is the value of the smaller number?

38 In college, next year's tuition will increase by 15% per credit. If this year's tuition in college was $660, what will it be next year?

37. An investment of $600 increases at a rate of 4% per year. Find the value of investment after 12 years. (Round your answer to the nearest dollar).

American Math Academy

PRACTICE TEST II ANSWER SHEET
CALCULATOR SECTION

1. Ⓐ Ⓑ Ⓒ Ⓓ
2. Ⓐ Ⓑ Ⓒ Ⓓ
3. Ⓐ Ⓑ Ⓒ Ⓓ
4. Ⓐ Ⓑ Ⓒ Ⓓ
5. Ⓐ Ⓑ Ⓒ Ⓓ
6. Ⓐ Ⓑ Ⓒ Ⓓ
7. Ⓐ Ⓑ Ⓒ Ⓓ
8. Ⓐ Ⓑ Ⓒ Ⓓ
9. Ⓐ Ⓑ Ⓒ Ⓓ
10. Ⓐ Ⓑ Ⓒ Ⓓ
11. Ⓐ Ⓑ Ⓒ Ⓓ
12. Ⓐ Ⓑ Ⓒ Ⓓ

13. Ⓐ Ⓑ Ⓒ Ⓓ
14. Ⓐ Ⓑ Ⓒ Ⓓ
15. Ⓐ Ⓑ Ⓒ Ⓓ
16. Ⓐ Ⓑ Ⓒ Ⓓ
17. Ⓐ Ⓑ Ⓒ Ⓓ
18. Ⓐ Ⓑ Ⓒ Ⓓ
19. Ⓐ Ⓑ Ⓒ Ⓓ
20. Ⓐ Ⓑ Ⓒ Ⓓ
21. Ⓐ Ⓑ Ⓒ Ⓓ
22. Ⓐ Ⓑ Ⓒ Ⓓ
23. Ⓐ Ⓑ Ⓒ Ⓓ

24. Ⓐ Ⓑ Ⓒ Ⓓ
25. Ⓐ Ⓑ Ⓒ Ⓓ
26. Ⓐ Ⓑ Ⓒ Ⓓ
27. Ⓐ Ⓑ Ⓒ Ⓓ
28. Ⓐ Ⓑ Ⓒ Ⓓ
29. Ⓐ Ⓑ Ⓒ Ⓓ
30. Ⓐ Ⓑ Ⓒ Ⓓ
31. Ⓐ Ⓑ Ⓒ Ⓓ
32. Ⓐ Ⓑ Ⓒ Ⓓ
33. Ⓐ Ⓑ Ⓒ Ⓓ
34. Ⓐ Ⓑ Ⓒ Ⓓ

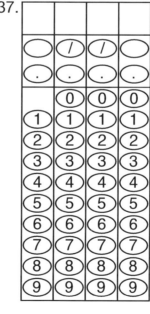

35. 36. 37. 38.

PRACTICE TEST II
NO CALCULATOR SECTION ANSWER KEY

1)	B
2)	B
3)	D
4)	C
5)	C
6)	A
7)	D
8)	C
9)	B
10)	C
11)	B
12)	B
13)	B
14)	A
15)	B
16)	36
17)	81.5
18)	3
19)	−2
20)	1/5 or 0.2

1. $\left(x+\dfrac{x}{2}\right)^2 = \left(x+\dfrac{x}{2}\right)\cdot\left(x+\dfrac{x}{2}\right)$ (Use the foil method)

$$= x^2 + \dfrac{x^2}{2} + \dfrac{x^2}{2} + \dfrac{x^2}{4}$$

$$= x^2 + x^2 + \dfrac{x^2}{4}$$

$$= 2x^2 + \dfrac{x^2}{4}$$

$$= \dfrac{9x^2}{4}$$

Correct Answer : B

2. $\sqrt{2} \cong 1.21$

$\sqrt{8} \cong 2.8$

$1.4 < x < 2.8$

Choice B is between $1.4 < x < 2.8$

Correct Answer : B

3.

	liters pure water	% water	total liters
80% water	x	.80	.80x
30% water	40	.30	.30(40)=12
60% water	x + 40	.60	.60(x+40)

From the last column, you get the equation
0.80x + 12 = 0.6(x + 40) Solve for x.

0.80x + 12 = 0.6x + 24

0.80x − 0.6x = 24 − 12

0.2x = 12

2x = 120

x = 60 liters.

Correct Answer : D

4. $2a + 3b = 18 \longrightarrow$ Multily by(−)then use elemenation method to find a and b.

$-2a - 3b = -18$

$\underline{+ \quad 3b - 5a = 11}$

$-7a = -7$

a = 1. Plug in one of the above equations and find b.

2(1) + 3b = 18

2 + 3b = 18

3b = 16

b = 16/3

$a - b = 1 - \dfrac{16}{3} = \dfrac{-13}{3}$

Correct Answer : C

5. Increasing = 168,000 − 120,000 = 48,000

Percentage of the increase

$$= \dfrac{48,000}{120,00} = \dfrac{48 \div 6}{120 \div 6} = \dfrac{8 \times 5}{20 \times 5} = \dfrac{40}{100} = 40\%$$

Correct Answer : C

6. $\dfrac{2}{x-3} = \dfrac{5}{2x-7}$ (Cross multiply)

2(2x − 7) = 5(x − 3)

4x − 14 = 5x − 15

−14 + 15 = 5x − 4x

1 = x

Correct Answer : A

7. $x^3 = 64,$

$x^3 = 4^3$

$x = 4$, then $x^2 = 4^2 = 16$

Correct Answer : D

8. Eggs $\longrightarrow$ 8x2 $= 16 = 2^4$

Milk $\longrightarrow$ 4x2^2 $= 16 = 2^4$

End of the shopping he pays total $= 2^4 + 2^4 = 2^a$

$2^4\,(1{+}1) = 2^a$

$2^4 \cdot 2^1 = 2^a$

$2^5 = 2^a$, $a = 5$

Correct Answer : C

9. $6^{\frac{1}{3}} = 2^{\frac{1}{3}} \cdot 3^{\frac{1}{3}}$, then

$$\frac{2^{\frac{1}{2}} \cdot 2^{\frac{1}{3}} \cdot 3^{\frac{1}{3}}}{3^{\frac{1}{3}} \cdot 2^{\frac{-1}{6}}} = \frac{2^{\frac{1}{2}} \cdot 2^{\frac{1}{3}}}{2^{\frac{-1}{6}}} = \frac{2^{\frac{5}{6}}}{2^{\frac{-1}{6}}} = 2^{\frac{5}{6} + \frac{1}{6}}$$

$$= 2^{\frac{6}{6}} = 2^1$$

Correct Answer : B

10.

24 feet

32 feet

The Perimeter of the garden is $2(24 + 32) =$ 112 feet

GCF of (24, 32) = 8 feet

Number of trees is $\dfrac{112}{8} = 14$

He pays at least 14x5 = \$70.

Correct Answer : C

11. If a is even number, and then a + 2 and a + 4 are also even number.

$$a + a + 2 + a + 4 = 42$$
$$3a + 6 = 42$$
$$3a = 36$$
$$a = 12$$

Half of smallest number : $\dfrac{12}{2} = 6$

Correct Answer : B

12. Since C is the center

$$m(A) = m(B) = 40°$$

Arc AE $= 80°$

Correct Answer : B

American Math Academy

13. $\dfrac{x^2}{9} - \dfrac{y^2}{4} = \left(\dfrac{x}{3} - \dfrac{y}{2}\right) \cdot \left(\dfrac{x}{3} + \dfrac{y}{2}\right)$

Correct Answer : B

14. $\dfrac{3x + 15 - 8}{7} = \dfrac{17 - 6 + x}{5}$

$\dfrac{3x + 7}{7} = \dfrac{11 + x}{5}$ (Cross multiply)

$5(3x + 7) = 7(11 + x)$

$15x + 35 = 77 + 7x$

$15x - 7x = 77 - 35$

$8x = 42$

$x = \dfrac{42}{8} = \dfrac{21}{4}$

Correct Answer : A

15. $\left(\dfrac{1+i}{1-i}\right)^{2018}$

$= \left(\dfrac{(1+i)(1+i)}{(1-i)1+i}\right)^{2018}$

$= \left(\dfrac{1+i+i+i^2}{1-i^2}\right)^{2018}$

$= \left(\dfrac{1+2i-1}{1+1}\right)^{2018} = \left(\dfrac{2i}{2}\right)^{2018}$

$= i^{2018}$

$= (i^2)^{1009} = (-1)^{1009} = -1$

Correct Answer : B

16. $3\alpha + 5\alpha = 96°$

$8\alpha = 96° \longrightarrow \alpha = 12° \longrightarrow 3\alpha = 3 \cdot 12 = 36°$

Correct Answer : 36°

17. Mean (average)

$= \dfrac{88 + 85 + 95 + 66 + 75 + 80}{6}$

$= 81.5$

Correct Answer : 81.5

18. $f(x) = x^2 - 2cx + 8$, if $f(x)$ polynomial is divisible by $x - 4$ then

$x - 4 = 0, \ x = 4$

$f(4) = 4^2 - 2c(4) + 8$

$0 = 4^2 - 2c(4) + 8$

$0 = 16 - 8c + 8$

$0 = 24 - 8c$

$8c = 24$

$c = 3$

Correct Answer : 3

American Math Academy

19. If $x = 1 - \sqrt{3}$ and $y = 1 + \sqrt{3}$, then

$$x \cdot y = (1 - \sqrt{3}) \cdot (1 + \sqrt{3})$$

$$= 1 - 3$$

$$= -2$$

Correct Answer : -2

20. $\sqrt[4]{0.0016} = \sqrt[4]{\dfrac{16}{10,000}}$

$$= \sqrt[4]{\left(\dfrac{2}{10}\right)^4}$$

$$= \dfrac{2}{10}$$

$$= \dfrac{1}{5}$$

Correct Answer : $\dfrac{1}{5}$ or 0.2

American Math Academy

PRACTICE TEST II
CALCULATOR SECTION ANSWER KEY

1)	A		20)	C
2)	B		21)	B
3)	B		22)	C
4)	C		23)	A
5)	A		24)	A
6)	C		25)	B
7)	A		26)	A
8)	C		27)	C
9)	D		28)	D
10)	A		29)	D
11)	D		30)	B
12)	D		31)	D
13)	B		32)	D
14)	C		33)	C
15)	C		34)	B
16)	D		35)	3.19×10^8
17)	B		36)	10
18)	B		37)	$961
19)	C		38)	$759

1. $\dfrac{\sqrt{3}\cdot\sqrt[3]{27}}{\sqrt[3]{8}\cdot\sqrt{2}} = \dfrac{\sqrt{3}\cdot\sqrt[3]{3^3}}{\sqrt[3]{2^3}\cdot\sqrt{2}} = \dfrac{\sqrt{3\cdot3}}{2\sqrt{2}} = \dfrac{3}{2\sqrt{2}}$

$\qquad = \dfrac{3\cdot(\sqrt{2})}{2\sqrt{2}\cdot(\sqrt{2})} = \dfrac{3\sqrt{2}}{4}$

Correct Answer : A

2. $A = \{-7,-6,-5,-4,-3,-2,-1,0,1,2,3,4,5,6\}$

$B = \{-9,-7,-5,-3,-1,3,5,7,9\}$

$s(A\cap B) = \{-7,-5,-3,-1,3,5\}$

Correct Answer : B

3. Julia $\longrightarrow$ 60%

Mike $\longrightarrow$ 30%

Peter $\longrightarrow$ 10%

Julia $\longrightarrow 500\cdot\dfrac{60}{100} = 300$ votes

Mike $\longrightarrow 500\cdot\dfrac{30}{100} = 150$ votes

Diffference between Julia and Mike

$300 - 150 = 150$ votes.

Correct Answer : B

4. $f(x) = 3x - 6$

$f(x) = 3x - 6 \longrightarrow f(2) = 3\cdot2 - 6 = 0$

Inverse function:

$y = 3x - 6$ (add 6 in both side)

$y + 6 = 3x$ (divided by 3 both side)

$\dfrac{y+6}{3} = x$ (change x to y for find inverse)

$f^{-1}(x) = \dfrac{x+6}{3} \longrightarrow f^{-1}(3) = \dfrac{3+6}{3} = \dfrac{9}{3} = 3$

$f(2) + f^{-1}(3) = 0 + 3 = 3$

Correct Answer : C

5. Probability of the selected odd:

$= \dfrac{P\,odd\,numbers}{total}$

$= \dfrac{5}{10} = \dfrac{1}{2}$

Correct Answer : A

6.

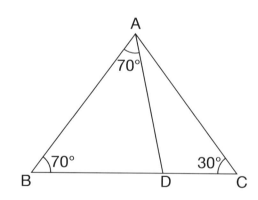

$140 + 30 = 170$

$\widehat{DAC} = 180 - 170$

$\widehat{DAC} = 10$

Correct Answer : C

7. If $\bigcirc = \triangle$, then

$x^2 - 2x + 1 = x2 - 1$

$-2x + 1 = -1$

$-2x = -2$

$x = 1$

Correct Answer : A

8. $g(x) = \dfrac{x}{2} + \dfrac{y}{3} = 1 \Longrightarrow 3x + 2y = 6$

$y = g(x) = \dfrac{6 - 3x}{2}$

$g(4) = \dfrac{6 - 12}{2} = -3$

$f(-3) = 3$

$f(3) = -3$

$f(g(4)) + f(3)$

$= 3 - 3$

$= 0$

Correct Answer : C

9. $\cos 30° \cdot \sin 60° \cdot \tan 60°$

$= \dfrac{\sqrt{3}}{2} \cdot \dfrac{\sqrt{3}}{2} \cdot \sqrt{3}$

$= \dfrac{3\sqrt{3}}{4}$

Correct Answer : D

10. Function graph intersect to x line three different points which are $-2, 0, 2$

So, equation has to be $f(x) = x(x - 2) \cdot (x + 2)$

Correct Answer : A

11. We know $|BD| = 27, |BC| = 15$

$|CD| = 27 - 15 = 12$ then $|CE| = 13$

$\sin\alpha = \dfrac{12}{13}$

$\cot\beta = \dfrac{15}{8}$

$\sin\alpha \cdot \cot\beta = \dfrac{12}{13} \cdot \dfrac{15}{8} = \dfrac{45}{26}$

Correct Answer : D

12. A) Between 1 and 2 months $\tan\alpha = 1$,

B) Between 2 and 5 months $\tan\beta = \dfrac{1}{3}$,

C) Between 1 and 1 months $\tan\alpha = 1$,

D) Between 5 and 6 months $\tan Q = 2$

Correct Answer : D

13. $\tan\alpha = \dfrac{2}{3}$

$(0,0)$ is satisfied;

$y - 0 = \dfrac{2}{3}(x - 0)$

$y = \dfrac{2}{3}x$

Correct Answer : B

American Math Academy

14. $(x + 8) \cdot (x + 11)$

$x^2 + 19x + 88$

Correct Answer : C

15. $f(x) = t(x + 2)(x - 4)(x + 7)$

So, $x + 7$ is a factor of $f(x)$.

Correct Answer : C

16. $f(a) = (a - 4)^2 + 11$

$g(a) = 2a + 2$

If $f(a) = g(a) \implies (a - 4)^2 + 11 = 2a + 2$

$a^2 - 8a + 16 + 11 = 2a + 2$

$a^2 - 10a + 25 = 0$

$(a - 5)^2 = 0$

$a = 5$

Correct Answer : D

17. $[\{(a + b) \div c\} \cdot d] - e = 3$

$[\{(12 + 18) \div 10\} \cdot 3] - e = 3$

$3 \cdot 3 - e = 3$

$9 - 3 = e$

$6 = e$

Correct Answer : B

18. total students: 30

total 5th grade: 6

% of 5th grade $= \dfrac{6}{30} = \dfrac{1}{5}$

$= 20\%$

Correct Answer : B

19. Total point: $1 \cdot 4 + 2 \cdot 7 + 3 \cdot 4 + 4 \cdot 9 + 5 \cdot 6$

$= 4 + 14 + 12 + 36 + 30$

$= 96$

Average of GPA $= \dfrac{\text{total points}}{\text{number of students}}$

$= \dfrac{96}{30} = \dfrac{32}{10} = 3.2$

Correct Answer : C

20. $\left(\dfrac{\sin\alpha}{\cos\alpha} \cdot \cos\alpha\right)^2 + \left(\sin\alpha \cdot \dfrac{\cos\alpha}{\sin\alpha}\right)^2 =$

$\sin\alpha^2 + \cos\alpha^2 = 1$

Correct Answer : C

21. $x^2 + x - 12 = 0$

$(x - 3)(x + 4) = 0$

$x - 3 = 0$, then $x = 3$

or

$x + 4 = 0$, then $x = -4$

The sum of the solutions $3 - 4 = -1$

Correct Answer : B

American Math Academy

22. $2a - 3b = 12 \longrightarrow$ multiply all equation by 5

$3a + 5b = 18 \longrightarrow$ multiply all equation by 3

$10a - \cancel{15b} = 60$

$+ \quad 9a + \cancel{15b} = 54$

$19a = 114$

$a = 6$

$b = 0$

$a - b = 6 - 0 = 6$

Correct Answer : C

23. $\dfrac{1}{a} = \dfrac{1}{b} + \dfrac{1}{c}$

$\dfrac{1}{a} = \dfrac{c + b}{bc}$ (cross multiply)

$ac + ab = bc$

$ac = bc - ab$

$ac = b(c - a)$

$\dfrac{ac}{c - a} = b$

Correct Answer : A

24. $x^2 + 4x - 8 = 0$

$x^2 + 4x = 8$

$(x + 2)^2 - 4 = 8$

$(x + 2)^2 = 12$

$x + 2 = \mp\sqrt{12}$

$x + 2 = \mp 2\sqrt{3}$

$x + 2 = \mp 2\sqrt{3}$

$x = -2 \mp 2\sqrt{3}$

Correct Answer : A

25. Number of students with no glasses $= \dfrac{18}{34} = \dfrac{9}{17}$

Correct Answer : B

26. Probability that the selected student is a girl

$= \dfrac{16}{34} = \dfrac{8}{17}$

Correct Answer : A

27. Probability that the selected student is no glasses and girls

$= \dfrac{6}{34} = \dfrac{3}{17}$

Correct Answer : C

28. Choice D does not represent linear relation because the domain is repeating.

Correct Answer : D

29. $\dfrac{1}{3} : \dfrac{1}{b}$ and $\dfrac{1}{18} : \dfrac{1}{12}$

$\dfrac{\frac{1}{3}}{\frac{1}{b}} = \dfrac{\frac{1}{18}}{\frac{1}{12}}$

$\dfrac{1}{3} \cdot \dfrac{b}{1} = \dfrac{1}{18} \cdot \dfrac{12}{1}$

$\dfrac{b}{3} = \dfrac{12}{18}$ $\quad 18b = 36$, $b = 2$

Correct Answer : D

30. $x^2 + ax - 10 = (x - 1) \cdot (bx + c)$

$x^2 + ax - 10 = bx^2 + cx - bx - c$

$x^2 = x^2 b$, $b = 1$

$ax = x(c - b)$, $a = c - b$

$-10 = -c$, $c = 10$

$a = c - b$

$a = 10 - 1 = 9$

$a + c = 9 + 10 = 19$

Correct Answer : B

31. $3^{2x-16} = 27^{x-6}$

$3^{2x-16} = 3^{3(x-6)}$

$3^{2x-16} = 3^{3x-18}$

$2x - 16 = 3x - 18$

$2 = x$

Correct Answer : D

32. $x - 3 = \sqrt{x - 3}$

$(x - 3)^2 = x - 3$

$x^2 - 6x + 9 = x - 3$

$x^2 - 7x + 12 = 0$

$(x - 3) \cdot (x - 4) = 0$

$x = 3$ or $x = 4$

Correct Answer : D

33. Only Choice C

can be Direct Variation

$y = kx$

Correct Answer : C

34. $\dfrac{81^2 \cdot 9^3}{3^{10}} = \dfrac{(3^4)^2 \cdot (3^2)^3}{3^{10}} = \dfrac{(3)^8 \cdot (3)^6}{310}$

$= \dfrac{(3)^{14}}{3^{10}} = 3^{14-10} = 3^4$

Correct Answer : B

35. Highest salary = Player A = 3.41×10^8

Lowest salary = Player B = 2.20×10^7

Difference from highest salary to lowest salary:

$3.41 \times 10^8 - 2.20 \times 10^7$

$= 10^7 (34.1 - 2.20)$

$= 31.9 \times 10^7 = 3.19 \times 10^8$

Correct Answer : 3.19 x 10^8

36. If two numbers have a ratio of 5 to 2, and they are positive integers, then can be represented by 5x and 2x.

Since they differ by 15:

$5x - 2x = 15$

$3x = 15$

$x = 5.$

Smaller number $= 2x = 2 \cdot 5 = 10$

Bigger number $= 5x = 5 \cdot 5 = 25$

Value of smaller number is 10.

Correct Answer : 10

37. $A = P(1 + r)^t$

$P = \$600$

$r = 0.04$

$t = 12$ years

$A = P(1 + r)^t$

$A = \$600(1 + 0.04)^{12}$

$A = \$600(1.04)^{12}$

$A = \$960.61...$

$A = \$961$

Correct Answer : \$961

38. Increasing tuition $\$660 \cdot \dfrac{15}{100} = \dfrac{9900}{100} = \$99$

Next year tuition total $= \$660 + \$99 = \$759$

Correct Answer : \$759

REFERENCE SHEET

Directions

For each question from 1 to 15, solve each problem, choose the best answer from the choices provided, and fill in the corresponding bubble on your answer sheet.

- For questions 16 to 20, solve the problem and enter your answer in the grid on the answer sheet.
- Refer to the directions before question 18 for how to enter your answers in the grid. You may use any available space for scratch work.

REFERENCE

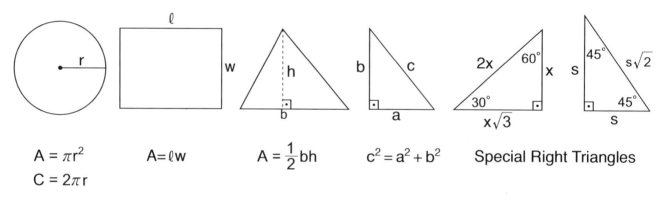

$A = \pi r^2$

$C = 2\pi r$

$A = \ell w$

$A = \dfrac{1}{2} bh$

$c^2 = a^2 + b^2$

Special Right Triangles

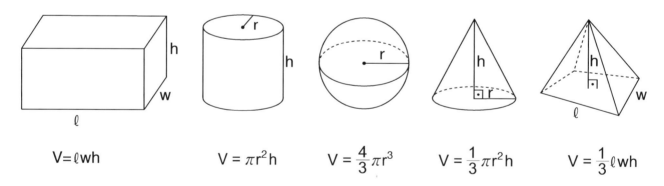

$V = \ell wh$

$V = \pi r^2 h$

$V = \dfrac{4}{3}\pi r^3$

$V = \dfrac{1}{3}\pi r^2 h$

$V = \dfrac{1}{3}\ell wh$

The number of degrees in a circle is 360.

The number of radians in a circle is 2π.

The sum of the measures in degrees of the angles of a triangle is 180.

1. If $x^3 = 64$, then find x^2.

A) 2

B) 4

C) 8

D) 16

2. If $4^{2x-3} = 8^{3x-7}$, then what is the value of x?

A) 1

B) 2

C) 3

D) 4

3. If $\dfrac{x}{y} = \dfrac{a}{b} = \dfrac{2}{3}$ and $y^2 - b^2 = 27$, then what is the value of $x^2 - a^2$?

A) 12

B) 20

C) 24

D) 25

American Math Academy

4. Let D, L and M be sets.

D = {a, b, c, d, e}

L = {b, c, e, q, r}

M = D∩L is given. According to these sets which of the following is equal to set L∪(D∩M)?

A) D

B) L

C) M∪D

D) L∪D

5. $\dfrac{2x-6}{4} = \dfrac{3x-5}{7}$

What is the solution to the equation above?

A) 5

B) 8

C) 11

D) 22

6.

$$\frac{|k+m|-|-2m|+|m-k|}{m-|k|}$$

From the above equation, if $0 > k > m$, what is the solution of the equation?

A) 2m

B) k

C) m + k

D) 0

7. If $y - 3x = 10$, then which of the following is equal to 6x?

A) $y - 5$

B) $2y - 5$

C) $2y - 20$

D) $2y + 20$

8.

X	1	2	3	4	5
Y	$\frac{9}{2}$	$\frac{13}{2}$	$\frac{17}{2}$	$\frac{21}{2}$	$\frac{25}{2}$

Which of the following equations relates y to x for the values in the table above? (In the x–y plane)

A) $\frac{3x}{2} + 4$

B) $7x + \frac{81}{4}$

C) $\frac{x}{2} + 9$

D) $2x + \frac{5}{2}$

9. If $a = 1 - 5i$ and $b = 1 + 5i$, then which of the following is equal to $a \cdot b$?

A) 10

B) 15

C) 25

D) 26

10.

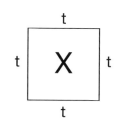

Area of square X is between 102 to 133.

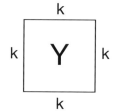

Area of square Y is between 244 to 283.

The side lengths and their area values are given above. If each side of the square has an integers value, what is the sum of $k + t$?

A) 25

B) 27

C) 30

D) 35

American Math Academy

Answer the following two questions according to the chart given below.

Subject	Correct	Incorrect
Math	120	40
Physics	60	15
Biology	45	15

The chart is about Frank's test correct and incorrect answers for each subject.

11. What is the percentage of correct answers of all math questions?

A) 50

B) 60

C) 75

D) 80

12. The following formula calculates the test correction average.

(Correct answers−incorrect answers) *2

Find the rate of $\dfrac{(Phy_{avg} + Bio_{avg})}{Math_{avg}}$.

A) $\dfrac{4}{5}$

B) $\dfrac{2}{3}$

C) $\dfrac{12}{13}$

D) $\dfrac{15}{16}$

13. The range of the polynomial function f is the set of real numbers less than or equal to 2. If the zeros of f are −5 and 3, which of the following could be the graph of y=f(x) in the xy−plane?

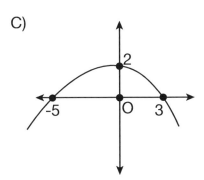

A)

B)

C)

D)

14. A{0, 1, 2, 3, 4, 5, 6, 7, 8, 9}

What is the probability of selecting an even number in set A?

A) $\dfrac{1}{2}$

B) $\dfrac{3}{4}$

C) $\dfrac{5}{6}$

D) $\dfrac{2}{3}$

16. If x and y are positive integers and, $\sqrt{x} = y^3 = 8$, then which of the following is the value of x − y?

15.

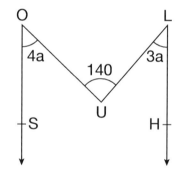

OS // LH

$m(\overparen{SOU}) = 4a, \angle(ULH) = 3a,$ and $\angle(OUL) = 140$

So what is the value of 2a?

A) 30

B) 40

C) 50

D) 80

17. What is the value of k if a line that passes through (4, 3) and (−2,k) has a slope of −1?

American Math Academy

18.
$$3x + y = 18$$
$$5x - 2y = 8$$

In the system of equations above, what is the value of $x + y$?

19. The perimeter of a rectangular garden is 43 cm. The width of the garden is 3 cm longer then 4 times the length. What is the length of the garden?

20. $\frac{1}{2}k - 5 + 3k = \frac{3}{2}(k + 4)$

What is the value of k in the equation shown above?

American Math Academy

1. Ⓐ Ⓑ Ⓒ Ⓓ   6. Ⓐ Ⓑ Ⓒ Ⓓ   11. Ⓐ Ⓑ Ⓒ Ⓓ
2. Ⓐ Ⓑ Ⓒ Ⓓ   7. Ⓐ Ⓑ Ⓒ Ⓓ   12. Ⓐ Ⓑ Ⓒ Ⓓ
3. Ⓐ Ⓑ Ⓒ Ⓓ   8. Ⓐ Ⓑ Ⓒ Ⓓ   13. Ⓐ Ⓑ Ⓒ Ⓓ
4. Ⓐ Ⓑ Ⓒ Ⓓ   9. Ⓐ Ⓑ Ⓒ Ⓓ   14. Ⓐ Ⓑ Ⓒ Ⓓ
5. Ⓐ Ⓑ Ⓒ Ⓓ   10. Ⓐ Ⓑ Ⓒ Ⓓ   15. Ⓐ Ⓑ Ⓒ Ⓓ

16.

	/	/	
.	.	.	.
	0	0	0
1	1	1	1
2	2	2	2
3	3	3	3
4	4	4	4
5	5	5	5
6	6	6	6
7	7	7	7
8	8	8	8
9	9	9	9

17.

	/	/	
.	.	.	.
	0	0	0
1	1	1	1
2	2	2	2
3	3	3	3
4	4	4	4
5	5	5	5
6	6	6	6
7	7	7	7
8	8	8	8
9	9	9	9

18.

	/	/	
.	.	.	.
	0	0	0
1	1	1	1
2	2	2	2
3	3	3	3
4	4	4	4
5	5	5	5
6	6	6	6
7	7	7	7
8	8	8	8
9	9	9	9

19.

	/	/	
.	.	.	.
	0	0	0
1	1	1	1
2	2	2	2
3	3	3	3
4	4	4	4
5	5	5	5
6	6	6	6
7	7	7	7
8	8	8	8
9	9	9	9

20.

	/	/	
.	.	.	.
	0	0	0
1	1	1	1
2	2	2	2
3	3	3	3
4	4	4	4
5	5	5	5
6	6	6	6
7	7	7	7
8	8	8	8
9	9	9	9

REFERENCE SHEET

Directions

For each question from 1 to 34, solve each problem, choose the best answer from the choices provided, and fill in the corresponding bubble on your answer sheet.

- For questions 35 and 38, solve the problem and enter your answer in the grid on the answer sheet.
- Refer to the directions before question 35 for how to enter your answers in the grid. You may use any available space for scratch work.

REFERENCE

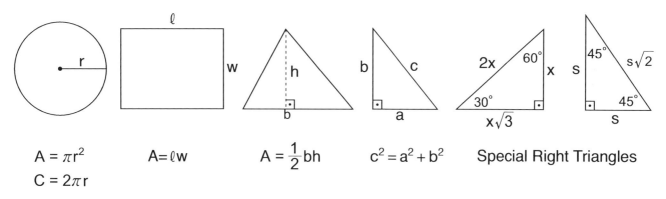

$$A = \pi r^2 \qquad A = \ell w \qquad A = \frac{1}{2}bh \qquad c^2 = a^2 + b^2 \qquad \text{Special Right Triangles}$$

$$C = 2\pi r$$

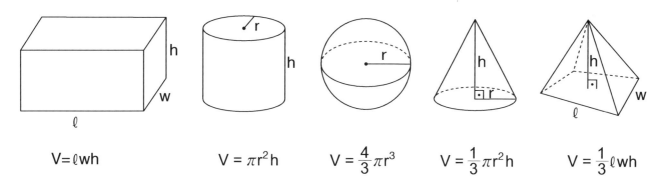

$$V = \ell wh \qquad V = \pi r^2 h \qquad V = \frac{4}{3}\pi r^3 \qquad V = \frac{1}{3}\pi r^2 h \qquad V = \frac{1}{3}\ell wh$$

The number of degrees in a circle is 360.

The number of radians in a circle is 2π.

The sum of the measures in degrees of the angles of a triangle is 180.

1. If $x = -2y + 16$ and $x - 3y = -4$, then what is the value of $\dfrac{y}{3}$?

A) 3

B) 4

C) $\dfrac{3}{4}$

D) $\dfrac{4}{3}$

2.
$$3a = 4b + 4$$
$$6a - 8b = 8$$

How many solutions does the system of equations show above?

A) Zero

B) 1

C) 2

D) Many/infinity

3. $2x - ky + 5 = 0$ if the slope of the equation is $\dfrac{3}{4}$, what is the value of k?

A) 3

B) 8

C) $\dfrac{3}{8}$

D) $\dfrac{8}{3}$

4.
$$f(x) = (x - 4)^2 + 11$$

The function g is defined by $g(x) = 2x + 2$

What is one possible value such that $f(a) = g(a)$?

A) 3

B) 5

C) 7

D) 9

5.
$$f(x) = ax^2 + bx + c.$$

If the function above has roots at -2, -5 and $(3,1)$ is satisfied by the function, find a and b?

A) $a = \dfrac{1}{40}$ $b = \dfrac{7}{40}$

B) $a = \dfrac{3}{40}$ $b = \dfrac{5}{40}$

C) $a = \dfrac{5}{40}$ $b = \dfrac{7}{40}$

D) $a = \dfrac{1}{40}$ $b = \dfrac{5}{40}$

American Math Academy

6.

Melisa has an electronic safe in her office. Her password is a four - digit number and the numbers are different from each other. What is the difference between her largest possible password and smallest possible password?

A) 8642

B) 8640

C) 8634

D) 8562

7.

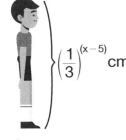 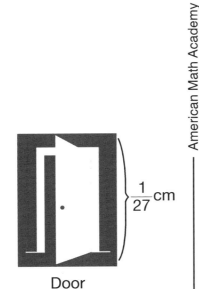

Child   Door

In the figure above if the childs height is more than the door height, what is the smallest value of x?

A) 7

B) 8

C) 9

D) 10

Use the following chart to answer questions 8 and 9.

Dealer Company has three different vehicle colors for cars and bikes. The colors are red, white and blue.

	Car	Bike
Red	30	15
White	40	10
Black	60	5

8. What is the probability of buying a white car from all cars?

A) $\dfrac{3}{4}$

B) $\dfrac{4}{13}$

C) 3

D) 4

9. What is the probability of buying a red car from all cars?

A) $\dfrac{3}{13}$

B) $\dfrac{13}{3}$

C) 3

D) 4

77

10. Simplify $\dfrac{x^2 - 8x + 15}{x^2 - 9} \div \dfrac{x^2 - 4x - 5}{x^2 + 3x}$

A) $x - 1$

B) $\dfrac{x}{x+1}$

C) $x + 1$

D) $\dfrac{x+1}{x-1}$

11. In ABC School, 60 student's favorite subject is science out of 480 students. Find the percent of students whose favorite subject is science?

A) 12.5%

B) 15%

C) 18%

D) 20%

12. Which of following graphs has no correlation?

A)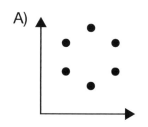

B)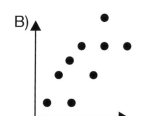

C)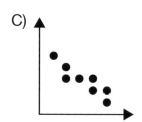

D)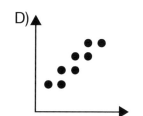

13. For what value of x is the equation
$x^2 - 3x - 5 = 0$ true?

A) $\dfrac{3 \pm \sqrt{29}}{2}$

B) $\dfrac{-1 \pm \sqrt{19}}{2}$

C) $\dfrac{-3 \pm \sqrt{26}}{4}$

D) $\dfrac{-3 \pm \sqrt{29}}{6}$

14. The table below shows the results of a survey on how students get to school. A circle graph is used to display the data. What percent of the graph represents the car transportation?

Number of Students	Transportation
180	School Bus
60	Car
20	Walk
40	Bike

A) 20%

B) 30%

C) 45%

D) 50%

15.

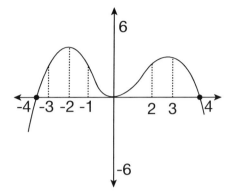

Which of the following could be the equation of the graph above?

A) $x \cdot (x - 3) \cdot (x + 3)$

B) $x^2 \cdot (x + 4) \cdot (x - 5)$

C) $x^2 \cdot (x^2 - 16)$

D) $x^2 \cdot (x + 4) \cdot (x - 3)$

17.

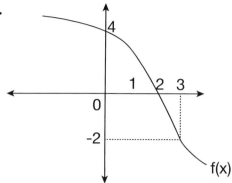

Using the above f(x) function, find the value of $f(0) + f^{-1}(-2) + f(3)$?

A)   5

B)   10

C)   12

D)   16

16.

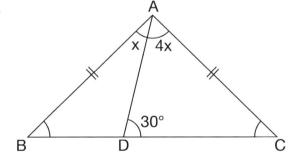

What is the value of x?

A)   20°

B)   40°

C)   60°

D)   80°

18. In a right triangle, one angle measures x°, where $\cos x° = \dfrac{5}{13}$.

What is the $\tan(90 - x°)$?

A) $\dfrac{12}{13}$

B) $\dfrac{5}{12}$

C) $\dfrac{7}{12}$

D) $\dfrac{13}{12}$

American Math Academy

19.

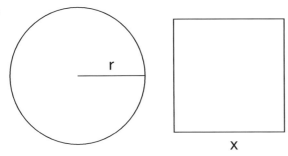

The area of the circle with radius r is equal to the area of the square with a side length of x. What is the ratio of the square's perimeter to the circle's circumference?

A) $\dfrac{2\sqrt{\pi}}{\pi}$

B) $\dfrac{\pi}{3}$

C) $\dfrac{3}{\pi}$

D) $\dfrac{2}{\pi}$

20. What is the vertex of the parabola $y = 3x^2 + 6x - 9$?

A) $f(x) = 3(x + 1)^2 - 12$

B) $f(x) = 3(x + 1)^2 - 6$

C) $f(x) = 3(x - 1)^2 - 4$

D) $f(x) = 3(x - 1)^2 - 9$

21. $\dfrac{1}{3}(3x - 9) + (x - 12) = ax + x + b$, What is the value of $a - b$?

A) 15

B) 16

C) 17

D) 18

22. The price of a book has been discounted 20%. The sale price is $60. What is the original price?

A) $25

B) $45

C) $65

D) $75

23. Simplify $\dfrac{x^2y + xy^2 - xy}{x^2 + xy - x}$

A) x

B) y

C) 2xy

D) −x

American Math Academy

24. If y variable inversely as x, and x = 6 when y = 8, find y when x = 10.

A) 3

B) 3.4

C) 4.8

D) 5.4

25. On the xy coordinate grid, a line K contains the points (1,3) and (−2,4). If the line L is parallel to line K at (2,1), which of the following is the equation of the line L?

A) $=-\dfrac{1}{2}x+\dfrac{5}{3}$

B) $=-\dfrac{2}{3}x+\dfrac{5}{3}$

C) $=-\dfrac{1}{3}x+\dfrac{3}{5}$

D) $=-\dfrac{1}{3}x+\dfrac{5}{3}$

26. x and y are integer numbers.
$$-1 < x < 8$$
$$2 < y < 6$$
What is the maximum value of $x^2 - y^2$?

A) 18

B) 36

C) 74

D) 81

27. For the following graph, which of the inequalities corresponds with it?

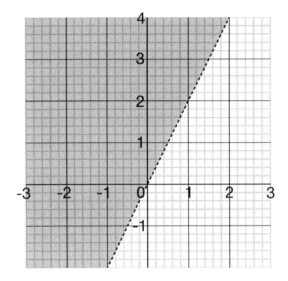

A) y > 2x

B) y < 2x

C) y = 2x

D) y = x

28. If 3x − 4y = 3, then find $\dfrac{27^x}{81^y}$.

A) 6

B) 9

C) 18

D) 27

American Math Academy

81

29. Which of the following graphs shows direct variation?

A)

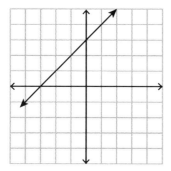

B)

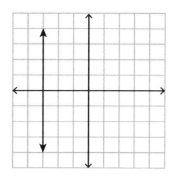

C)

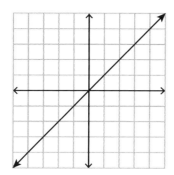

D)

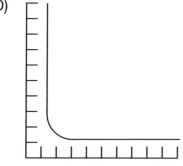

30.

$$(81x^8)^{\frac{1}{4}}$$

Which of the following equations is equivalent to the expression above?

A) x^2

B) $3x^2$

C) $\frac{1}{2}x^2$

D) $5x^2$

31. $P(x - 2) = x^2 + 3x - 10$, then find $P(3)$.

A) 10

B) 20

C) 30

D) 40

32. If a ratio of $\frac{2}{5} : \frac{1}{4}$ is equal to $\frac{2}{7} : \frac{b}{8}$, what is the value of b?

A) $\frac{5}{7}$

B) $\frac{6}{7}$

C) $\frac{8}{7}$

D) $\frac{10}{7}$

American Math Academy

33. If $P = \dfrac{N}{N+F}$, then find N in terms of P and F.

A) $\dfrac{PF}{1-P}$

B) $\dfrac{F}{P-1}$

C) PF

D) $P(F-1)$

35.

3x-4   2x $x - \dfrac{1}{2}$

A   B   C   D

Note: Figure not drawn to scale

on $\overline{AD}$ above, AB = CD. What is the length of $\overline{AD}$?

34. In the xy–plane, the graph of function g (x) has x–intercepts at 2,0,and −4.

Which of the following could define g (x)?

A) $3x^3 - 6x^2 + 24x$

B) $3x^3 + 12x^2 + 24x$

C) $3x^3 + 6x^2 - 24x$

D) $3x^3 - 12x^2 - 24x$

36. In the xy–plane, the point (3, 5) lies on the graph of the function h. If $h(x) = x^2 - c$, where c is a constant, what is the value of c?

American Math Academy

37. $\dfrac{3x-1}{(x-2)^2} - \dfrac{3}{x-2}$

The expression above is equivalent to $\dfrac{k}{(x-2)^2}$, where k is a positive constant and $x \neq 2$. What is the value of k?

38. An airplane traveled 1.5×10^2 miles per hour for 0.5×10^2 hours. How far did the airplane travel?

American Math Academy

84

PRACTICE TEST III ANSWER SHEET
CALCULATOR SECTION

1. (A) (B) (C) (D)   13. (A) (B) (C) (D)   24. (A) (B) (C) (D)
2. (A) (B) (C) (D)   14. (A) (B) (C) (D)   25. (A) (B) (C) (D)
3. (A) (B) (C) (D)   15. (A) (B) (C) (D)   26. (A) (B) (C) (D)
4. (A) (B) (C) (D)   16. (A) (B) (C) (D)   27. (A) (B) (C) (D)
5. (A) (B) (C) (D)   17. (A) (B) (C) (D)   28. (A) (B) (C) (D)
6. (A) (B) (C) (D)   18. (A) (B) (C) (D)   29. (A) (B) (C) (D)
7. (A) (B) (C) (D)   19. (A) (B) (C) (D)   30. (A) (B) (C) (D)
8. (A) (B) (C) (D)   20. (A) (B) (C) (D)   31. (A) (B) (C) (D)
9. (A) (B) (C) (D)   21. (A) (B) (C) (D)   32. (A) (B) (C) (D)
10. (A) (B) (C) (D) 22. (A) (B) (C) (D)   33. (A) (B) (C) (D)
11. (A) (B) (C) (D) 23. (A) (B) (C) (D)   34. (A) (B) (C) (D)
12. (A) (B) (C) (D)

35.

36.

37.

38.

PRACTICE TEST III
NO CALCULATOR SECTION ANSWER KEY

1)	D
2)	C
3)	A
4)	B
5)	C
6)	D
7)	C
8)	D
9)	D
10)	B
11)	C
12)	D
13)	C
14)	A
15)	B
16)	62
17)	9
18)	10
19)	3.7
20)	5.5

1. If $x^3 = 64$, then $x^3 = 4^3$, $x = 4$

$x^2 = 4^2 = 16$

Correct Answer : D

2. $4^{2x-3} = 8^{3x-7}$

$2^{2(2x-3)} = 2^{3(3x-7)}$

$2^{4x-6} = 2^{9x-21}$

$4x - 6 = 9x - 21$

$-6 + 21 = 9x - 4x$

$15 = 5x$

$3 = x$

Correct Answer : C

3. $\dfrac{x^2}{y^2} = \dfrac{a^2}{b^2} = \dfrac{4}{9}$ (Cross multiply)

$9x^2 = 4y^2 \longrightarrow y^2 = \dfrac{9x^2}{4}$

$9a^2 = 4b^2 \longrightarrow b^2 = \dfrac{9}{4}a^2$

if $y^2 - b^2 = 27$

$\dfrac{9x^2}{4} - \dfrac{9}{4}a^2 = 27$

$\dfrac{9x^2 - 9a^2}{4} = 27$

$\dfrac{9(x^2 - a^2)}{4} = 27$

$x^2 - a^2 = \dfrac{27 \cdot 4}{9} = 12$

Correct Answer : A

4. $M = D \cap L = \{b, c, e\}$ then $D \cap M = \{b, c, e\}$

So; $L \cup (D \cap M) = \{b, c, e, q, r\} \cup \{b, c, e\} = L$

Correct Answer : B

5. $\dfrac{2x-6}{4} = \dfrac{3x-5}{7}$ (Cross multiply)

$7(2x - 6) = 4(3x - 5)$

$14x - 42 = 12x - 20$

$14x - 12x = 42 - 20$

$2x = 22$

$x = 11$

Correct Answer : C

6. If $m < k < 0$, then

$|k + m| = -k - m$

$|-2m| = -2m$

$|m - k| = -m + k$

$|k| = -k$

$= \dfrac{-k + m + 2m - m + k}{1 + k} = \dfrac{0}{1 + k} = 0$

Correct Answer : D

American Math Academy

7. If $y - 3x = 10$, then $3x = y - 10$

So, $6x = 2(3x) = 2(y-10) = 2y - 20$

Correct Answer : C

8. $\left.\begin{array}{c}\left(1, \dfrac{9}{2}\right) \\ \left(1, \dfrac{13}{2}\right)\end{array}\right\}$ Use this 2 points to find slope.

$\text{Slope} = \dfrac{y_2 - y_1}{x_2 - x_1}$

$\text{Slope} = \dfrac{\dfrac{13}{2} - \dfrac{9}{2}}{2 - 1} = \dfrac{\dfrac{4}{2}}{2 - 1} = \dfrac{2}{1} = 2$

Slope point form:

$y - y_1 = m(x - x_1)$

$y - \dfrac{9}{2} = 2(x - 1)$

$y = 2x - 2 + \dfrac{9}{2}$

$y = 2x + \dfrac{5}{2}$

Correct Answer : D

9. $a = 1 - 5i$ and $b = 1 + 5i$, then

$a \cdot b = (1 - 5i) \cdot (1 + 5i)$

$= 1 - 25i^2$

$= 1 + 25$

$= 26$

Correct Answer : D

10. t is one side of square of X

$102 < t^2 < 133$

t must be 11

k is one side of square of Y

$244 < k^2 < 283$

k must be 16

$t + k = 11 + 16 = 27$

Correct Answer : B

11. Total math questions $= 120 + 40$

$= 160$

160 ⟍ 120
100 ⟋ x
$x = \dfrac{100 \cdot 120}{160} = 75\%$

Correct Answer : C

12. $\text{Phy}_{avg} = (60 - 15) \times 2 = 90$

$\text{Bio}_{avg} = (45 - 15) \times 2 = 60$

$\text{Math}_{avg} = (120 - 40) \times 2 = 160$

$\dfrac{(\text{Phy}_{avg} + \text{Bio}_{avg})}{\text{Math}_{avg}} = \dfrac{90 + 60}{160} = \dfrac{15}{16}$

Correct Answer : D

American Math Academy

13. (0, 2) Is satisfied and

$x = -5$ and $x = 3$

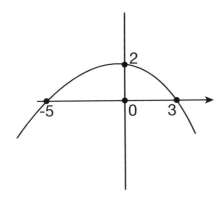

Correct Answer : C

14. Even numbers are 0,2,4,6,and, 8.

Probability of the selecting even number

$= \dfrac{5}{10} = \dfrac{1}{2}$

Correct Answer : A

15. Since $OS \parallel LH$ $4a + 3a = 140$

$7a = 140$

$a = 20$, then $2a = 40$

Correct Answer : B

16. If x and y are positive integers and

$\sqrt{x} = y^3 = 8$.

$\sqrt{x} = 8$, then $x = \mp 64$ since

x is positive then $x = 64$

$y^3 = 8$, then $y = 2$

$x - y = 64 - 2 = 62$

Correct Answer : 62

17. (4, 3), (−2, k) and slope $= -1$

$\text{Slope} = \dfrac{y_2 - y_1}{x_2 - x_1}$

$\text{Slope} = \dfrac{k - 3}{-2 - 4} = \dfrac{k - 3}{-6}$

$-1 = \dfrac{k - 3}{-6}$

$6 = k - 3$, $6 + 3 = k$

$9 = k$

Correct Answer : 9

American Math Academy

18. $3x + y = 18 \longrightarrow$ multiply all equations by 2

$5x - 2y = 8 \longrightarrow$ keep equation same

$6x + 2y = 36$

$\underline{\ \ 5x - 2y = 8}$

$+$

$11x = 44$

$x = 4$, then plug in 4 for x and find y.

$5x - 2y = 8$

$5(4) - 2y = 8$

$20 - 2y = 8$

$20 - 8 = 2y$

$12 = 2y$

$6 = y$

$x + y = 4 + 6 = 10$

Correct Answer : 10

20. $\dfrac{1}{2}k - 5 + 3k = \dfrac{3}{2}(k + 4)$

$\dfrac{1}{2}k + 3k - 5 = \dfrac{3}{2}k + \dfrac{3(4)}{2}$

$\dfrac{7k}{2} - 5 = \dfrac{3k}{2} + 6$

$\dfrac{7k}{2} - \dfrac{3k}{2} = 6 + 5$

$\dfrac{4k}{2} = 11$

$k = \dfrac{22}{4} = 5.5$

Correct Answer : 5.5

19. Perimeter of a rectangular garden $= 43$ cm

Perimeter $= 2L + 2W = 43$cm

$W = 4L + 3$

$2L + 2(4L + 3) = 43$

$2L + 8L + 6 = 43$

$10L = 43 - 6$

$10L = 37$

$L = 3.7$

Correct Answer : 3.7

PRACTICE TEST III
CALCULATOR SECTION ANSWER KEY

1)	D		20)	A
2)	D		21)	B
3)	D		22)	D
4)	B		23)	B
5)	A		24)	C
6)	A		25)	D
7)	C		26)	C
8)	B		27)	A
9)	A		28)	D
10)	B		29)	C
11)	A		30)	B
12)	A		31)	C
13)	A		32)	D
14)	A		33)	A
15)	C		34)	C
16)	B		35)	6
17)	A		36)	4
18)	B		37)	5
19)	A		38)	7,500 miles

1. $x + 2y = 16 \longrightarrow$ multiply by $(-)$ then use substitute method.

$$-x - 2y = -16$$
$$+ \quad x - 3y = -4$$
$$\overline{ \quad -5y = -20}$$

$y = 4$, then $\dfrac{y}{3}$ is $\dfrac{4}{3}$

Correct Answer : D

2. $3a = 4b + 4 \longrightarrow 3a - 4b = 4$

$6a - 8b = 8 \longrightarrow$ divide by 2 all the equations $\longrightarrow 3a - 4b = 4$

Since both equations are equivalent the system of equations has many/infinitely solutions.

Correct Answer : D

3. $2x - ky + 5 = 0 \longrightarrow$ from this equation the slope is $\dfrac{2}{k}$.

$\dfrac{2}{k} = \dfrac{3}{4}$ (cross multiply)

$3k = 8$

$k = \dfrac{8}{3}$

Correct Answer : D

4. $f(a) = (a - 4)^2 + 11$

$g(a) = 2a + 2$

If $f(a) = g(a) \Longrightarrow (a - 4)^2 + 11 = 2a + 2$

$a^2 - 8a + 16 + 11 = 2a + 2$

$a^2 - 8a + 27 = 2a + 2$

$a^2 - 10a + 25 = 0$

$(a - 5)^2 = 0$

$a = 5$

Correct Answer : B

5. $f(x) = t(x + 2) \cdot (x + 5)$, and $(3, 1)$ is satisfied that;

$1 = t(3 + 2) \cdot (3 + 5)$

$1 = t \cdot (5) \cdot (8)$

$1 = t \cdot 40$

$t = \dfrac{1}{40}$

So;

$f(x) = \dfrac{1}{40} \cdot (x + 2) \cdot (x + 5)$

$\Longrightarrow \dfrac{1}{40} \cdot (x^2 + 7x + 10)$

$\Longrightarrow \dfrac{x^2}{40} + \dfrac{7x}{40} + \dfrac{1}{4} = ax^2 + bx + c$

$a = \dfrac{1}{40}, b = \dfrac{7}{40}$

Correct Answer : A

6. Largest possible password: 9876

Smallest possible password: 1234

$9876 - 1234 = 8642$

Correct Answer : A

7. $\frac{1}{27} = 3^{-3}$, then

$$= \left(\frac{1}{3}\right)^{(x-5)} = 3^{5-x}$$

Since the child height is more than the door height

$3^{5-x} < 3^{-3}$,

$5 - x < -3$

$8 < x$ smallest possible value of x is 9

Correct Answer : C

8. Probability of buying a white car

$$= \frac{40}{30+40+60} = \frac{40}{130} = \frac{4}{13}$$

Correct Answer : B

9. Probability of buying a red car

$$= \frac{30}{30+40+60} = \frac{30}{130} = \frac{3}{13}$$

Correct Answer : A

10. $\frac{x^2-8x+15}{x^2-9} \div \frac{x^2-4x-5}{x^2+3x}$

$$\frac{(x-5)(x-3)}{(x-3)(x+3)} \cdot \frac{x(x+3)}{(x-5)(x+1)}$$

$$= \frac{x}{x+1}$$

Correct Answer : B

11. Percent of students whose favorite subject

is science $= \frac{60}{480} = \frac{1}{8} = 12.5\%$

Correct Answer : A

12. No Correlation

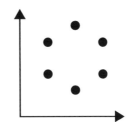

Correct Answer : A

13. $x^2 - 3x - 5 = 0$

$$x^2 - 3x = 5$$

$$\left(x - \frac{3}{2}\right)^2 - \frac{9}{4} = 5$$

$$\left(x - \frac{3}{2}\right)^2 = \frac{29}{4}$$

$$x - \frac{3}{2} = \mp\sqrt{\frac{29}{4}}$$

$$x = \mp\frac{\sqrt{29}}{2} + \frac{3}{2}$$

$$x = \frac{\mp\sqrt{29}+3}{2}$$

Correct Answer : A

American Math Academy

14. $\dfrac{\text{Car}}{\text{Total}} = \dfrac{6\cancel{0}}{30\cancel{0}} = \dfrac{6}{30}$

$\qquad = \dfrac{1 \times 20}{5 \times 20} = \dfrac{20}{100}$

$\qquad = 20\%$

Correct Answer : A

15. The graph's zeros are x = 0, x = 4, x = −4 but x = 0 is twice zeros so;

$f(x) = x^2 \cdot (x - 4) \cdot (x + 4)$

$\quad = x^2 \cdot (x^2 - 16)$

Correct Answer : C

16.

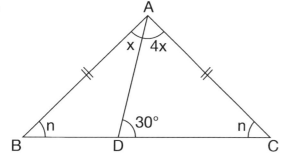

$x + n = 30°$

$5x + 2n = 180° \quad x = 40°$

Correct Answer : B

17. f(0) = 4

$\quad f^{-1}(-2) = 3$, then f(3) = −2

$\qquad f(0) + f^{-1}(2) + f(3) = 4 + 3 - 2 = 5$

Correct Answer : A

18.

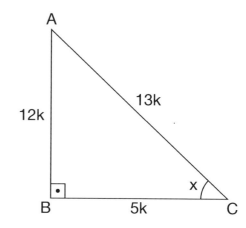

$\tan(90 - x°) = \cot x° = \dfrac{5k}{12k} = \dfrac{5}{12}$

Correct Answer : B

19. $\qquad$ Are of circle $= \pi r^2$

$\qquad$ Are of square $= x^2$

$\qquad\qquad x^2 = \pi r^2$, then $x = r\sqrt{\pi}$

$\qquad$ Perimeter of square $= 4r\sqrt{\pi}$

$\qquad$ Circum frence of circle $= 2\pi r$

$\dfrac{\text{Perimeter of square}}{\text{Circum frence of circle}} = \dfrac{4\cancel{r}\sqrt{\pi}}{2\pi\cancel{r}}$

$\qquad\qquad\qquad = \dfrac{2\sqrt{\pi}}{\pi}$

Correct Answer : A

American Math Academy

94

20. $y = 3x^2 + 6x - 9$

$y = 3(x^2 + 2x) + 9$

$y = 3(x + 1)^2 - 3 - 9$

$y = 3(x + 1)^2 - 12$

Correct Answer : A

21. $\frac{1}{3}(3x - 9) + (x - 12) = ax + x + b$

$x - 3 + x - 12 = ax + x + b$

$2x - 15 = x(a + 1) + b$

$2 = a + 1$

$1 = a$

$-15 = b$

$a - b = 1 - (-15)$

$= 16$

Correct Answer : B

22. Original price $= 100x$.

20% discount from original price

$= \frac{20 \cdot 100x}{100} = 20x$.

Sales price $= 100x - 20x = \$60$

$80x = \$60$

$x = \frac{60}{80} = \frac{6}{8} = \frac{3}{4}$.

Original price $= 100x = 100 \cdot \frac{3}{4} = \frac{300}{4} = 75$.

Correct Answer : D

23. $\dfrac{x^2y + xy^2 - y}{x^2 + xy - x}$

$= \dfrac{xy(x + y - 1)}{x(x + y - 1)}$

$= \dfrac{xy}{x} = y$

Correct Answer : B

24. Inverse Variation: $y \cdot x = k$

$6 \cdot 8 = k$

$48 = k$

$yx = k$

$y \cdot 10 = 48$

$y = 4.8$

Correct Answer : C

American Math Academy

25. $(1,3)$ and $(-2,4)$

$$\text{Slope} = \frac{y_2 - y_1}{x_2 - x_1}$$

$$m = \frac{4-3}{-2-1} = -\frac{1}{3}$$

If $m_1 \,//\, m_2$, then $m_1 = m_2$

$$m_2 = -\frac{1}{3}, (2,1) \rightarrow \text{use the point-slope form}$$

$$y - y_1 = m(x - x_1)$$

$$y - 1 = -\frac{1}{3}(x - 2)$$

$$y - 1 = -\frac{1}{3}x + \frac{2}{3}$$

$$y = -\frac{1}{3}x + \frac{2}{3} + 1$$

$$y = -\frac{1}{3}x + \frac{5}{3}$$

Correct Answer : D

26. Since x and y are integer numbers.

$-1 < x < 8$

$2 < y < 6$

Maximum value of x is: 7

Maximum value of y is: 5

$x^2 + y^2 = 7^2 + 5^2 = 49 + 25 = 74$

Correct Answer : C

27. From the graph when x = 0, y < 4

Only Choice A will give you the correct answer.

Correct Answer : A

28. If $3x + 4y = 3$, and $\frac{27^x}{81^y}$.

$$\frac{27^x}{81^y} = \frac{3^{3x}}{3^{4y}} = 3^{3x-4y} = 3^3 = 27$$

Correct Answer : D

29. Only Choice C

can be Direct Variation

$y = kx$

Correct Answer : C

30. $(81x^8)^{\frac{1}{4}} = (3^4 x^8)^{\frac{1}{4}} = 3x^2$

Correct Answer : B

31. $P(x - 2) = x^2 + 3x - 10$, then plug 5 in x to find P(3).

$$P(5 - 2) = 5^2 + 3(5) - 10$$

$$P(3) = 25 + 15 - 10$$

$$P(3) = 40 - 10$$

$$P(3) = 30$$

Correct Answer : C

32. If the ratio of $\frac{2}{5} : \frac{1}{4}$ is equal to $\frac{2}{7} : \frac{b}{8}$

$\frac{8}{5} = \frac{17}{7b}$ (Cross multiply)

$56b = 80$

$b = \frac{80}{56} = \frac{10}{7}$

Correct Answer : D

33. $P = \frac{N}{N+F}$ (Cross multiply)

$P(N + F) = N$

$PN + PF = N$

$PF = N - PN$

$PF = N(1 - P)$

$\frac{PF}{1-P} = N$

Correct Answer : A

34. If the g(x) function has x− intercept at 2, 0, and −4, then x − 2, x and x + 4 must be factor of g(x).

$g(x) = kx(x - 2)(x + 4) \longrightarrow$ which k is a constant

$g(x) = kx(x^2 + 2x - 8) \longrightarrow$ FOIL

$g(x) = k(x^3 + 2x^2 - 8x) \longrightarrow$ Distributive property

Since the leading coefficient is 3 in each answer choice, k must be 3.

$g(x) = 3(x^3 + 2x^2 - 8x)$

$g(x) = 3x^3 + 6x^2 - 24x$

Correct Answer : C

35. $AB = 3x - 4$

$CD = x - \frac{1}{2}$

If $AB = CD$, then

$3x - 4 = x - \frac{1}{2}$

$3x - x = 4 - \frac{1}{2}$

$2x = \frac{7}{2}$

$x = \frac{7}{4}$

$AD = 3x - 4 + 2x + x - \frac{1}{2}$

$AD = 6x - \frac{9}{2}$

$AD = 6\left(\frac{7}{4}\right) - \frac{9}{2}$

$AD = \frac{42}{4} - \frac{9}{2} = \frac{42 - 18}{4}$

$AD = \frac{42 - 18}{4} = \frac{24}{4} = 6$

Correct Answer : 6

36. $h(x) = x^2 - c$,$(3,5) \longrightarrow$ plug in this point to function for find c.

$h(3) = 3^2 - c$

$5 = 9 - k$

$c = 9 - 5$

$c = 4$

Correct Answer : 4

37. $\dfrac{3x-1}{(x-2)^2} - \dfrac{3}{x-2} = \dfrac{k}{(x-2)^2}$ (make their denominators same)

$$\dfrac{3x-1}{(x-2)^2} - \dfrac{3(x-2)}{(x-2)^2} = \dfrac{k}{(x-2)^2}$$

$$\dfrac{3x-1-3(x-2)}{(x-2)^2} = \dfrac{k}{(x-2)^2} \quad \text{(take out denominators)}$$

$$3x-1-3x+6 = k$$

$$-1+6 = k$$

$$5 = k$$

Correct Answer : 5

38. Distance = Rate x Time

Distance = $(1.5 \times 10^2)(0.5 \times 10^2)$

Distance = 0.75×10^4

Distance = $0.75(10,000)$

Distance = 7,500 miles.

Correct Answer : 7,500 miles.

American Math Academy

REFERENCE SHEET

Directions

For each question from 1 to 15, solve each problem, choose the best answer from the choices provided, and fill in the corresponding bubble on your answer sheet.

- For questions 16 to 20, solve the problem and enter your answer in the grid on the answer sheet.
- Refer to the directions before question 18 for how to enter your answers in the grid. You may use any available space for scratch work.

REFERENCE

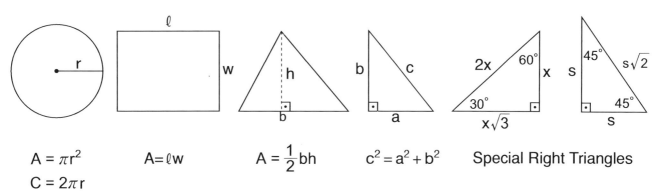

$A = \pi r^2$

$A = \ell w$

$A = \frac{1}{2} bh$

$c^2 = a^2 + b^2$

Special Right Triangles

$C = 2\pi r$

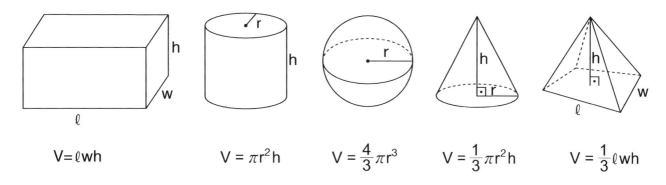

$V = \ell wh$

$V = \pi r^2 h$

$V = \frac{4}{3} \pi r^3$

$V = \frac{1}{3} \pi r^2 h$

$V = \frac{1}{3} \ell wh$

The number of degrees in a circle is 360.

The number of radians in a circle is 2π.

The sum of the measures in degrees of the angles of a triangle is 180.

1. If $x^{\frac{1}{3}} = 64$, then find $\frac{x}{2}$.

A) 2^{15}

B) 2^{17}

C) 2^{18}

D) 2^{20}

2. If $9^{(2x-3)} = 27^{(3x-7)}$, then what is the value of x?

A) 1

B) 2

C) 3

D) 4

3.
$$\frac{x-6}{3} = \frac{2x-7}{4}$$

What is the solution to the equation above?

A) -2

B) -3

C) $-\frac{2}{3}$

D) $-\frac{3}{2}$

4. If $3y - \frac{x}{4} = 10$, then which of the following is equal to $\frac{x}{2}$?

A) $6y - 20$

B) $3y - 10$

C) $y - 20$

D) $6y + 20$

5. Which of the following is equal to $\frac{4}{1+i\sqrt{3}}$?

A) $1 - i\sqrt{3}$

B) $1 + i\sqrt{3}$

C) 1

D) 3i

6.
$$a^2 - b^2 = 36$$

$$\frac{1}{a-b} + \frac{1}{a+b} = \frac{2}{9}$$

From the above equations, if a and b are integers, what is the value of a?

A) 3

B) 4

C) 5

D) 6

American Math Academy

100

7. Tricio is $6\frac{3}{4}$ years old, Laurie is $6\frac{1}{2}$ years old, Jim is 6.25 years old. Mark is 6.5 years old. Which two children have the same age?

A) Laurie and Mark

B) Tricio and Jim

C) Mark and Jim

D) Laurie and Tricio

9. A fitness center has two membership plans. One is a $23 membership fee and $7 per visit and another one is only per visit fees of $13.Which of the following systems of equations can be used to determine the fitness center membership plans?

A) $y = 7 + 23x$
$y = 13$

B) $y = 23 + 7x$
$y = 13x$

C) $y = 13$
$y = 23 + 7x$

D) $y = 13x$
$y = 23x + 7$

8. If $A = \sqrt{5}, B = \sqrt{6}, C = 3,$ and $D = \sqrt{20},$ what is the value of $|A - B| + |C - B| + |D - C|$?

A) $\sqrt{5}$

B) 0

C) $-\sqrt{5}$

D) 6

10. A→↗ (multiply by 6) ↘→↗ (substract 5) ↘→↗ (multiply by 2) ↘→↗ (divided by 7) ↘→14

A number is applied step by step in the direction of arrows and the result is 14. Which of following is true for A?

A) A is a prime number.

B) A is a even number.

C) A is a perfect square.

D) A is a negative number.

American Math Academy

11. If x and y are positive integers and

$$y = x^2 + 9$$

$$y = 7x - 3$$

Which of following could be value of x?

A) 2

B) 4

C) 6

D) 8

12.

$$\frac{k}{2km} = \frac{1}{k+m}$$

From the above equation what is the value of m in terms of k?

A) k^2

B) $k^2 + 1$

C) $k^2 - 1$

D) k

13. If x hour is equivalent to y minutes, of the following, which best represents the relationship between x and y?

A) x = y

B) x = 30y

C) x = 60y

D) x = 120y

14.

$$(x - 3)^2 + (y + 7)^2 = 16$$

If a circle in the xy−plane has the equation above, what is the radius of the circle?

A) 3

B) 4

C) 5

D) 7

15.

AB // DE

What is the value of x?

A) 120°

B) 140°

C) 150°

D) 160°

American Math Academy

16. If x and y are positive integers and $\sqrt{x} = y^4 = 16$, then which of the following is the value of $x - y$?

17. What is the value of k if a line that passes through $(-7, 3)$ and $(2, k)$ has a slope of 1?

18.

$$\frac{1}{2}x + y = 18$$

$$x - \frac{3}{2}y = 8$$

In the system of equations above, what is the value of $x + y$?

19. Melissa's monthly electrical bill was $125. Due to a rate decrease, her monthly bill is now $110. To the nearest to tenth of a percent, by what percent did the amount of the customers electrical bill decrease?

20.

$$k - 9 + \frac{5k}{2} = \frac{1}{2}k + 7$$

What is the value of k in the equation shown above?

American Math Academy

PRACTICE TEST IV ANSWER SHEET
NO CALCULATOR SECTION

1. Ⓐ Ⓑ Ⓒ Ⓓ   6. Ⓐ Ⓑ Ⓒ Ⓓ   11. Ⓐ Ⓑ Ⓒ Ⓓ
2. Ⓐ Ⓑ Ⓒ Ⓓ   7. Ⓐ Ⓑ Ⓒ Ⓓ   12. Ⓐ Ⓑ Ⓒ Ⓓ
3. Ⓐ Ⓑ Ⓒ Ⓓ   8. Ⓐ Ⓑ Ⓒ Ⓓ   13. Ⓐ Ⓑ Ⓒ Ⓓ
4. Ⓐ Ⓑ Ⓒ Ⓓ   9. Ⓐ Ⓑ Ⓒ Ⓓ   14. Ⓐ Ⓑ Ⓒ Ⓓ
5. Ⓐ Ⓑ Ⓒ Ⓓ   10. Ⓐ Ⓑ Ⓒ Ⓓ   15. Ⓐ Ⓑ Ⓒ Ⓓ

16.

17.

18.

19.

20.

REFERENCE SHEET

Directions

For each question from 1 to 34, solve each problem, choose the best answer from the choices provided, and fill in the corresponding bubble on your answer sheet.

- For questions 35 and 38, solve the problem and enter your answer in the grid on the answer sheet.
- Refer to the directions before question 35 for how to enter your answers in the grid. You may use any available space for scratch work.

REFERENCE

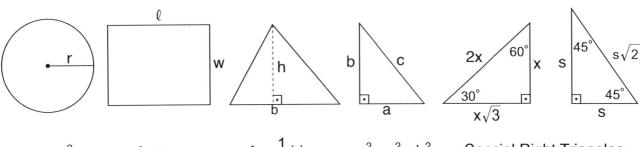

$A = \pi r^2$ $A = \ell w$ $A = \dfrac{1}{2}bh$ $c^2 = a^2 + b^2$ Special Right Triangles

$C = 2\pi r$

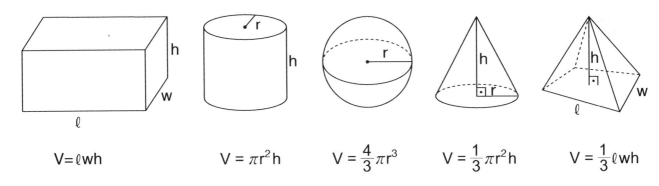

$V = \ell wh$ $V = \pi r^2 h$ $V = \dfrac{4}{3}\pi r^3$ $V = \dfrac{1}{3}\pi r^2 h$ $V = \dfrac{1}{3}\ell wh$

The number of degrees in a circle is 360.

The number of radians in a circle is 2π.

The sum of the measures in degrees of the angles of a triangle is 180.

1. Suppose that x is an integer such that $\frac{x}{4}$ is 10 greater than $\frac{x}{5}$. Which of the following is the value of x?

A) 180

B) 190

C) 200

D) 210

2.

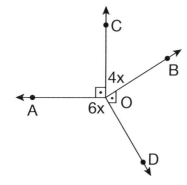

From the figure $\angle(BOC)= 4x$, and $\angle(AOD)=6x$. What is the value of x?

A) 12°

B) 16°

C) 18°

D) 20°

3. What are the solutions of x in the following system of equations?

$$x^2 - 4x + y = 14$$
$$5x - y = 6$$

A) (−1, 4)

B) (4, 5)

C) (−4, −5)

D) (−5, 4)

4. What is the solution(s) for y in the following equation?

$$\frac{12}{\sqrt[5]{y}} = 6$$

A) 16 and −16

B) 32 and −32

C) 16 only

D) 32 only

5.
$$f(x) = \begin{cases} -2x+3, & x<0 \\ x^2+4, & x\geq0 \end{cases}$$

From the above function, find $f(1) + f(-2)$?

A) 7

B) 8

C) 9

D) 12

American Math Academy

6. In the following cylinder shape, if the volume of the cylinder 72π cm³, find the radius of the cylinder.

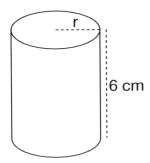

6 cm

A) $\sqrt{3}$ cm

B) $2\sqrt{3}$ cm

C) $3\sqrt{3}$ cm

D) 6 cm

7. If a is the average of 8k and 10, b is the average of 6k and 10, and c is the average of 10k and 40, what is the average of a, b, and c in terms of k?

A) 4k + 20

B) 4k – 15

C) 4k + 15

D) 4k + 10

8. Two classes took a science test. The first class had 20 students and their average test score was 90%. The second class had 24 students and their average score was 85%. If the teacher combined the test scores of both classes, what is the average of both classes together? Round your answer to the nearest percent.

A) 82%

B) 83%

C) 86%

D) 87%

9. Formula A: $A = \dfrac{3x + y}{7}$

Formula B: $A = \dfrac{2x + 5y}{12}$

Base on the formulas, what is the value of x in terms of y?

A) $x = \dfrac{23}{22}y$

B) $x = \dfrac{22}{23}y$

C) $x = 23y$

D) $x = 22y$

10. If $\dfrac{x}{4} = 7$ and $x + y = 35$, what is the value of $x - y$?

A) 18

B) 21

C) 24

D) 27

11. The athlete moves from A to B and the distance is $\frac{1}{4}$ of the total. When the athlete arrives at C, the distance equals to $\frac{1}{3}$ of the total. When the athlete arrives at B, the time is 8:50AM. When the athlete arrives at C, the time is 9:00AM. What time is it when the athlete arrives to D?

A) 10:00 A.M.

B) 10:20 A.M.

C) 9:40 A.M.

D) 9:50 A.M.

12. If a,b and c are positive integers and;

a + b is odd

a · c is even

b · c is odd

Which one of the following is must be an odd number?

A) a^2b

B) $a + 2b$

C) b^3c

D) $a + 2c$

13. $\frac{7\sin x° + 2\cos x°}{4\cos x° + 5\sin x°} = \frac{3}{5}$, then what is cot x°?

A) 7

B) 9

C) 10

D) 11

14. $$\frac{|x-y|}{|y-z|} = 6$$

From the above equation, if x = 18 and y = 6, then which of the following could be the value of z?

A) 3

B) 6

C) 8

D) 9

American Math Academy

108

15.

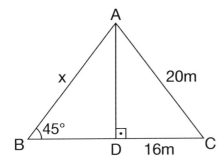

$|AC| = 20m$

$|DC| = 16m$

$m(\overparen{ABD}) = 45°$

What is tle length of x?

A) 8m

B) $8\sqrt{2}\,m$

C) $12\sqrt{2}\,m$

D) 16m

16.

$$\overset{3x-1}{\underset{A \quad\quad B}{\cdots\cdots}}\overset{2x}{\underset{C}{\cdots\cdots}}\overset{x+8}{\underset{D}{\cdots\cdots}}$$

Note: Figure not drawn to scale.

On $|AD|$ above, and $|AB| = 2|CD|$.

$$|AB| = 3x - 1$$

$$|BC| = 2x$$

$$|CD| = x + 8$$

What is the length of $|AD|$?

A) 103

B) 105

C) 107

D) 109

17. In the xy–plane the point (3, 8) lies on the graph of the function f.

$f(x) = t - 3x^2$, Where t is a constant. What is the value of t?

A) 31

B) 33

C) 35

D) 37

18. $\boxed{X}\xrightarrow{-5}\square\xrightarrow{\div 3}\square\xrightarrow{+10}\square\xrightarrow{x2}\boxed{50}$

According to the figure above, what is x?

A) 50

B) 40

C) 30

D) 20

19. The operation sequence is given below and it has a rule.

$3 \otimes 4 = 22$

$5 \otimes 2 = 20$

$7 \otimes 8 = 66$

What is the solution of $6 \otimes 7$?

A) 40

B) 44

C) 50

D) 52

20.
.A   .B   .C   .D

There are four markets on the same road and there are four points on the road.

Distances between these points are given below.

A			
X	B		
90	Y	C	
160	110	Z	D

If the distance between A and C is 90 feet, according to the above table, what is the value of X, Y and Z?

	X	Y	Z
A)	30	40	50
B)	50	60	80
C)	50	40	70
D)	30	50	60

American Math Academy

Answer the following two questions according to the bar graph and circle graphs that are given below.
The bar graph and circle graph below describe the same data.

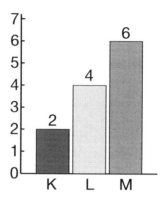
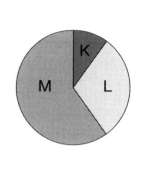

21. What is the measure of the angle L, in degrees in the circle graph?

A) 100°

B) 110°

C) 120°

D) 130°

22. What is the measure of the angle M, in degrees in the circle graph?

A) 100°

B) 180°

C) 200°

D) 300°

23. If x, y and z are real numbers and;

$$x^3 \cdot y^2 > 0$$

$$x^2 \cdot z > 0$$

$$y^3 \cdot z < 0$$

Which of the following must be true?

A) $+, +, +$

B) $-, +, -$

C) $+, -, -$

D) $+, -, +$

24.

State	Weather
Washington	W
Texas	T
New York	N

The graph given above is about the weather of these three states.

- The temperature in Washington is below zero
- The temperature of NY's absolute value is bigger than Washington's absolute value.
- Texas has the highest temperature and is bigger than zero.

According to the information's above which of the following is true?

I. $W \cdot T \cdot N > 0$

II. $W + N < 0$

III. When $N > 0$ then $W \cdot N < 0$

A) I

B) II

C) III

D) I, II

Use the following chart to answer questions 25 to 28

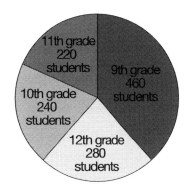

The above graph gives the number of students in different classes in high school. 9th grade has a total of 460 students, 10th grade has a total of 240 students, 11th grade has a total of 220 students and 12th grade has a total of 280 students.

25. According to the graph, what is the center angle measure corresponding to 12th grade?

A) 32°

B) 64°

C) 72°

D) 84°

American Math Academy

26. According to the graph, what is the center angle measure corresponding to 10th grade?

A) 35°

B) 68°

C) 72°

D) 88°

27. According to the graph, what percent of students are in 10th grade?

A) 15%

B) 20%

C) 35%

D) 40%

28. According to the graph what percent of students are in 12th grade?

A) 23.$\overline{3}$

B) 33.$\overline{3}$

C) 43.$\overline{3}$

D) 53.$\overline{3}$

29.

Playlist Number	Song Name	Song's Minute
1	S	3
2	O	2.5
3	U	2
4	L	1.5
5	M	4

The graph gives Jennifer's playlist and their minutes. The playlist plays nonstop from the 1st song to the 5th song and turns to the 1st song again. This situation is being repeated. When U song is playing, Jennifer is leaving school and she is coming home 1 hour later. Which song will play when Jennifer is arriving at home?

A) S

B) O

C) U

D) L

American Math Academy

30.

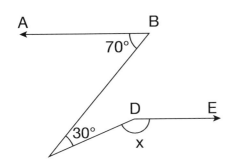

AB // DE

What is the value of x?

A) 120 °

B) 140 °

C) 150 °

D) 160°

31.

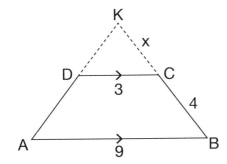

If DC // AB in the above figure, what is the value of x?

A) 2

B) 4

C) 6

D) 8

32. The radius of a cylinder is increased by 25% and its height is decreased by 20%. What is the effect on the volume of the cylinder?

A) It is decreased by 50%

B) It is decreased by 25%

C) It is increased by 25%

D) It is increased by 50%

33. A new copy machine can print 120 pages per hour, and an older copy machine can print 80 pages per hour. How many minutes will two copy machines working together, take to copy a total of 360 pages?

A) 72

B) 96

C) 108

D) 120

34. $\dfrac{a^{2m}}{a^{22}} = a^{18}$ and $a^{3n} = a^{45}$, what is the value of

$m \cdot n$?

A) 200

B) 300

C) 400

D) 500

35. If the ratio of the circumference to the area of a circle is 2 to 3, what is the radius of the circle?

37. $3^y + 3^y + 3^y = 81^2$, then find y.

36. $2^x \cdot 2^x \cdot 2^x \cdot 2^x = 64^2$, then find x.

38 If $x = 7y$ and $\dfrac{x}{2} - \dfrac{y}{3} = 57$, then find x.

American Math Academy

PRACTICE TEST IV ANSWER SHEET
CALCULATOR SECTION

1. (A) (B) (C) (D)   13. (A) (B) (C) (D)   24. (A) (B) (C) (D)
2. (A) (B) (C) (D)   14. (A) (B) (C) (D)   25. (A) (B) (C) (D)
3. (A) (B) (C) (D)   15. (A) (B) (C) (D)   26. (A) (B) (C) (D)
4. (A) (B) (C) (D)   16. (A) (B) (C) (D)   27. (A) (B) (C) (D)
5. (A) (B) (C) (D)   17. (A) (B) (C) (D)   28. (A) (B) (C) (D)
6. (A) (B) (C) (D)   18. (A) (B) (C) (D)   29. (A) (B) (C) (D)
7. (A) (B) (C) (D)   19. (A) (B) (C) (D)   30. (A) (B) (C) (D)
8. (A) (B) (C) (D)   20. (A) (B) (C) (D)   31. (A) (B) (C) (D)
9. (A) (B) (C) (D)   21. (A) (B) (C) (D)   32. (A) (B) (C) (D)
10. (A) (B) (C) (D)   22. (A) (B) (C) (D)   33. (A) (B) (C) (D)
11. (A) (B) (C) (D)   23. (A) (B) (C) (D)   34. (A) (B) (C) (D)
12. (A) (B) (C) (D)

35. 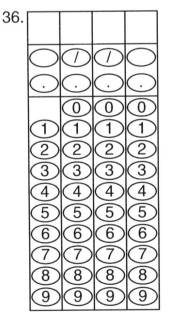   36.   37.   38.

PRACTICE TEST IV
NO CALCULATOR SECTION ANSWER KEY

1)	B
2)	C
3)	D
4)	A
5)	A
6)	B
7)	A
8)	A
9)	B
10)	C
11)	B
12)	D
13)	C
14)	B
15)	B
16)	254
17)	12
18)	28
19)	12%
20)	16/3

1. $x^{\frac{1}{3}} = 64$, then $x^{\frac{1}{3}} = 4^3 \longrightarrow$ multily each power

by 3 to find x

$$x^{\frac{1(3)}{3}} = 4^{3(3)}$$

$$x = 4^9$$

$$\frac{x}{2} = \frac{4^9}{2^1} = \frac{(2^2)^9}{2^1} = \frac{2^{18}}{2^1} = 2^{18-1} = 2^{17}$$

Correct Answer : B

2. $9^{2x-3} = 27^{3x-7}$

$(3^2)^{2x-3} = (3^3)^{3x-7} \longrightarrow$ use power to power rule.

$(3)^{4x-6} = (3)^{9x-21} \longrightarrow$ since base are same power must be equal.

$4x - 6 = 9x - 21 \longrightarrow$ simplify

$21 - 6 = 9x - 4x$

$\quad 15 = 5x$

$\quad\quad 3 = x$

Correct Answer : C

3. $\dfrac{x-6}{3} = \dfrac{2x-7}{4}$ (cross multiply)

$4(x - 6) = 3(2x - 7)$

$4x - 24 = 6x - 21$ (simplify)

$-24 + 21 = 6x - 4x$

$-3 = 2x$

$-\dfrac{3}{2} = x$

Correct Answer : D

4. $3y - \dfrac{x}{4} = 10$

$3y - 10 = \dfrac{x}{4} \longrightarrow$ multiply both sides by 2.

$2(3y - 10) = \dfrac{x}{4}(2)$

$6y - 20 = \dfrac{x}{2}$

Correct Answer : A

5. $\dfrac{4}{1 + i\sqrt{3}} = \dfrac{4}{1 + i\sqrt{3}}\left(\dfrac{1 - i\sqrt{3}}{1 - i\sqrt{3}}\right)$

$\quad = \dfrac{4 - 4i\sqrt{3}}{1 - 3i^2} = \dfrac{4 - 4i\sqrt{3}}{1 + 3}$

$\quad = \dfrac{4 - 4i\sqrt{3}}{4} = 1 - i\sqrt{3}$

$\quad\quad\quad i^2 = -1$

Correct Answer : A

6. $\dfrac{1}{a-b} + \dfrac{1}{a+b} = \dfrac{2}{9}$

$\quad = \dfrac{1}{a-b}\left(\dfrac{a+b}{a+b}\right) + \dfrac{1}{a+b}\left(\dfrac{a-b}{a-b}\right) = \dfrac{2}{9}$

$\dfrac{a+b+a-b}{a^2-b^2} = \dfrac{2}{9}$

$\dfrac{2a}{36} = \dfrac{2}{9}$

$18a = 72$

$a = 4$

Correct Answer : B

American Math Academy

117

7. Tricio: $6\dfrac{3}{4} = \dfrac{27}{4}$

Laurie: $6\dfrac{1}{2} = \dfrac{13}{2}$

Jim: $6\dfrac{1}{4} = \dfrac{25}{4}$

Mark: $6\dfrac{1}{2} = \dfrac{13}{2}$

Laurie and Mark

Correct Answer : A

8. $|\sqrt{5} - \sqrt{6}| + |3 - \sqrt{6}| + |\sqrt{20} - 3| =$

$-\sqrt{5} + \sqrt{6} + 3 - \sqrt{6} + \sqrt{20} - 3 = \sqrt{5}$

Correct Answer : A

9. First plan: $23 membership fee and $7 per visit $\longrightarrow$ convert to the equation.

$y = \$23 + 7x$

Second plan: only per visit fee of $13 $\longrightarrow$ convert to the equation.

$y = 13x$ (no membership fee)

Correct Answer : B

10. The inverse of an operation is gets you back to the number you started with.

$14 . 7 = 98$

$\dfrac{98}{2} = 49$

$49 + 5 = 54$

$\dfrac{54}{6} = 9$

$A = 9$ and 9 is a perfect square so option C is true for A.

Correct Answer : C

11.

$y = x^2 + 9$

$y = 7x - 3$

Use substation method to find x.

$x^2 + 9 = 7x - 3$

$x^2 - 7x + 12 = 0$

$(x - 3)(x - 4) = 0$

$x = 3$ or $x = 4$

Correct Answer : B

12. $\dfrac{k}{2km} = \dfrac{1}{k+m}$ (Cross multiply)

$k(k + m) = 2km$

$k^2 + km = 2km$

$k^2 = km$

$k = m$

Correct Answer : D

American Math Academy

13. If x hour is equivalent to y minutes:

x = 60y

Correct Answer : C

14. $(x-h)^2 + (y-k)^2 = r^2$

$(x-3)^2 + (y+7)^2 = 16$

$r^2 = 16$

$r = 4$

Correct Answer : B

15.

Since AB // DE

$m + 30° = 70°$ $m = 40°$

$m + x = 180°$

$40° + x = 180°$ $x = 140°$

Correct Answer : B

16. since x and y are positive integers:

$\sqrt{x} = y^4 = 16$, then

$\sqrt{x} = 16$, x=256

$y^4 = 16$,

$y^4 = 2^4$

$y = 2$

$x - y = 256 - 2 = 254$

Correct Answer : 254

17. Line that passes through $(-7, 3)$ and $(2,k)$ has a slope of 1.

$Slope = \dfrac{y_2 - y_1}{x_2 - x_1} = \dfrac{k-3}{2-(-7)}$

$\dfrac{k-3}{9} = 1$

$k - 3 = 9$

$k = 12$

Correct Answer : 12

18. $\frac{1}{2}x + y = 18$ (multiply all equations by -2.)

$-x - 2y = -36$

$x - \frac{3}{2}y = 8$

$+$ _____

$-\frac{7}{2}y = -28$

$y = 8$

plug in y in one of the above equations and then find x.

$\frac{1}{2}x + y = 18$

$\frac{1}{2}x + 8 = 18$

$\frac{1}{2}x = 18 - 8$

$\frac{1}{2}x = 10$

$x = 20$

$x + y = 8 + 20$

$= 28$

Correct Answer : 28

19. Decrease: $\dfrac{\text{decrease amount}}{\text{original amount}} = \dfrac{\$125 - \$110}{\$125}$

$= \frac{15}{125} = \frac{3}{25}$

$= \frac{3}{25} \times \frac{4}{4} = \frac{12}{100} = 12\%$

Correct Answer : 12%

20. $k - 9 + \frac{5k}{2} = \frac{1}{2}k + 7$

$\frac{7k}{2} - 9 = \frac{1}{2}k + 7$

$\frac{7k}{2} - \frac{1}{2}k = 7 + 9$

$\frac{6k}{2} = 16$

$3k = 16$

$k = \frac{16}{3}$

Correct Answer : $\frac{16}{3}$

American Math Academy

PRACTICE TEST IV
CALCULATOR SECTION ANSWER KEY

1)	C		20)	C
2)	C		21)	C
3)	D		22)	B
4)	D		23)	D
5)	D		24)	C
6)	B		25)	D
7)	D		26)	C
8)	D		27)	B
9)	D		28)	A
10)	B		29)	A
11)	B		30)	B
12)	C		31)	A
13)	C		32)	C
14)	C		33)	C
15)	C		34)	B
16)	D		35)	3
17)	C		36)	3
18)	A		37)	7
19)	D		38)	Y = 18

PRACTICE TEST IV
CALCULATOR SECTION SOLUTIONS

1. $\dfrac{x}{4} = \dfrac{x}{5} + 10$

$\dfrac{x}{4} - \dfrac{x}{5}$ (Find LCD of both numbers)

$\dfrac{5x}{20} - \dfrac{4x}{20} = 10$

$\dfrac{x}{20} = 10$

$x = 200$

Correct Answer : C

2. $6x + 4x + 90° + 90° = 360°$

$10x = 360° - 180°$

$10x = 180°$

$x = 18°$

Correct Answer : C

3. $x^2 - 4x + y = 14$ and $5x - y = 6$, then $y = 5x - 6$

$x^2 - 4x + 5x - 6 = 14$

$x^2 + x - 20 = 0$

$(x + 5)(x - 4) = 0$

$x = -5$ or $x = 4$

$x = (-5, 4)$

Correct Answer : D

4. $\dfrac{12}{\sqrt[5]{y}} = 6$

$\sqrt[5]{y} = \dfrac{12}{6}$

$\sqrt[5]{y} = 2$, $\sqrt[5]{y^5} = 2^5$

$y = 2^5 = 32$

Correct Answer : D

5. $f(x) = x^2 + 4$, when $x \geq 0$

$f(1) = 1^2 + 4 = 5$

$f(x) = -x + 5$, when $x < 0$

$f(-2) = -(-2) + 5 = 2 + 5 = 7$

$f(1) + f(-2) = 5 + 7 = 12$

Correct Answer : D

6.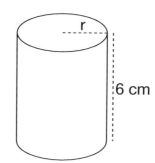

Volume of cylinder $= \pi r^2 h$

$\pi r^2 \cdot 6cm = 72\pi cm^3$

$r^2 \cdot 6cm = 72cm^3$

$r^2 = \dfrac{72cm^3}{6cm}$, $r^2 = 12cm^2$

$r = 2\sqrt{3}\,cm$

Correct Answer : B

American Math Academy

122

7.
$$a = \frac{8k + 10}{2} = 4k + 5$$

$$b = \frac{6k + 10}{2} = 3k + 5$$

$$c = \frac{10k + 40}{2} = 5k + 20$$

Average of a, b, and $c = \frac{a + b + c}{3}$

$$= \frac{4k + 5 + 3k + 5 + 5k + 20}{3}$$

$$= \frac{12k + 30}{3} = 4k + 15$$

Correct Answer : D

8.
$$x = \frac{20(0.90) + 24(0.85)}{44}$$

$$x = \frac{18 + 20 \cdot 4}{44}$$

$$x = \frac{38.4}{44}$$

$$x \approx 87\%$$

Correct Answer : D

9. Formula A = Formula B

$$\frac{3x + y}{7} = \frac{2x + 5y}{12} \quad \text{(Cross Multiply)}$$

$$36x + 12y = 14x + 35y$$

$$36x - 14x = 35y - 12y$$

$$22x = 23y$$

$$x = \frac{23}{22}y$$

Correct Answer : A

10.
$$\frac{x}{4} = 7 \ , \ x = 28$$

$$28 + y = 35$$

$$y = 35 - 28$$

$$y = 7$$

$$x - y = 28 - 7 = 21$$

Correct Answer : B

11. Let Distance $|AD| = 12x$

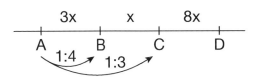

so $|AB| = 3x$

$|AC| = 4x$

$|CD| = 8x$

$|BC| = x$

When the athlete arrive from B to C since diffrence between the time is 10 minutes.

x distance 10 minutes

8x distance 80 minutes

9:00 a.m + 80minutes = 10:20 A.M

Correct Answer : B

12. If b · c is odd then b and c have to be odd. Then if a · c is even and we know c is odd so a has to be even. Thus a^2b, a + 2b , and a + 2c is even but b^3c is odd.

Correct Answer : C

13. $35\sin x° + 10\cos x° = 12\cos x° + 15\sin x°$

$20\sin x° = 2\cos x°$

$10\sin x° = \cos x°$

$10 = \dfrac{\cos x°}{\sin x°}$

$\cot x° = \dfrac{\cos x°}{\sin x°} = 10$

Correct Answer : C

14. $\dfrac{|x-y|}{|y-z|} = 6$

If $x = 18$ and $y = 6$, then plug in equation.

$\dfrac{|18-6|}{|6-z|} = 6$

$\dfrac{|12|}{|6-z|} = 6$, $\dfrac{12}{|6-z|} = 6$

$|6-z| = 2$

$6 - z = \pm 2$

$6 \pm 2 = z$

$6 + 2 = z$ or $6 - 2 = z$

$8 = z$ or $4 = z$

Correct Answer : C

15. $|AD|^2 + 16^2 = 20^2$

$|AD| = 12m$

$s(\widehat{BAC}) = 45°$, then $|BD| = 12m$

$|AB| = x = 12\sqrt{2}\,m$

Correct Answer : C

16. $|AB| = 2|CD|$, then $3x - 1 = 2(x+8)$

$3x - 1 = 2x + 16 \longrightarrow x = 17$

$|AD| = 3x - 1 + 2x + x + 8$

$|AD| = 6x + 7 \longrightarrow |AD| = 6 \cdot 17 + 7 = 109$

Correct Answer : D

17. We know $x = 3$ and $y = 8$, then $f(x) = t - 3x^2$

$f(3) = t - 3 \cdot (3)^2$

$8 = t - 27$

$t = 35$

Correct Answer : C

18. Starting from back then;

$50 \div 2 = 25$

$25 - 10 = 15$

$15 \cdot 3 = 45$

$45 + 5 = 50$, then x is 50.

Correct Answer : A

19. The rule of the operation is

$x \otimes y = x \cdot y + 10$

Check

$3 \otimes 4 = 3 \cdot 4 + 10 = 22$

$5 \otimes 2 = 5 \cdot 2 + 10 = 20$

$7 \otimes 8 = 7 \cdot 8 + 10 = 66$

Then

$6 \otimes 7 = 6 \cdot 7 + 10 = 52$

Correct Answer : D

American Math Academy

20.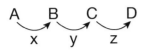

$AC = 90$, $x + y = 90$

$AD = 160$, $x + y + z = 160$, $z = 70$

$BO = 110$, $y + z = 110$

$y + 70 = 110$ $y = 40$

$AC = 90$, $x + y = 90$

$x + 40 = 90$ $x = 50$

Correct Answer : C

21.

$K = 2t$

$L = 4t$

$M = 6t$

$2t + 4t + 6t = 12t$

$12t = 360°$

$t = 30°$

$L = 120°$

Correct Answer : C

22.

$K = 2t$

$L = 4t$

$M = 6t$

$2t + 4t + 6t = 12t$

$12t = 360°$

$t = 30°$

$M = 6t = 6 \cdot 30 = 180°$

Correct Answer : B

23. If $x^3 \cdot y^2 > 0$ so y^2 is always positive then $x > 0$

If $x^2 \cdot z > 0$ so x^2 is always positive then $z > 0$

If $y^3 \cdot z < 0$ so we knows $z > 0$ then $y < 0$

Correct Answer : D

24.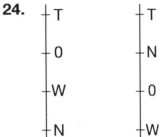

From above number line

I. is false

II. is false

III. is true

Correct Answer : C

25. Total students in school $= 1200$

Total students in 12th grade $= 280$

If 1200 students 360°

280 students x°

―――――――――――――

$1200 \cdot x = 280 \cdot 360°$

$x = 84°$

Correct Answer : D

American Math Academy

26. Total students in school = 1200

Total students in 10th grade = 240

If 1200 students 360°

240 students x°

_____

$1200 \cdot x = 240 \cdot 360$

$x = 72°$

Correct Answer : C

27. Total students in school = 1200

Total students in 10th grade = 240

If 1200 students 100%

240 students x %

_____

$1200 \cdot x = 240 \cdot 100$

$x = 20\%$

Correct Answer : B

28. Total students in school = 1200

Total students in 12th grade = 280

If 1200 students 100%

280 students 100%

_____

$1200 \cdot x = 280 \cdot 100$

$x = 23.\overline{3}$

Correct Answer : A

American Math Academy

29. $U + L + M = 2 + 1.5 + 4 = 7.5$ minutes

$S + O + U + L + M = 13$ minutes

$7.5 + 13 + 13 + 13 + 13 = 59.5$ minutes

$59.5 + x = 60$ minutes. $x = 0.5$ minutes

Correct Answer : A

30.

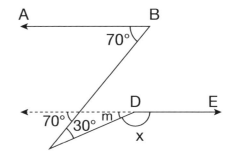

since AB // DE

$m + 30° = 70°$ $m = 40°$

$m + x = 180°$

$40° + x = 180°$ $x = 140°$

Correct Answer : B

31.

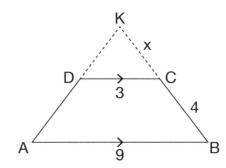

From similarity theorem

$\dfrac{x}{x+4} = \dfrac{3}{9}$ $\dfrac{x}{x+4} = \dfrac{1}{3}$ (cross multiply)

$3x = x + 4$

$3x - x = 4$

$2x = 4$

$x = 2$

Correct Answer : A

32. Suppose $\quad r = 4 \quad V = \pi r^2$

$\qquad h = 5 \quad V = \pi \cdot 16 \cdot 5 = 80\pi$

$\qquad r \longrightarrow 25\%$ increase $r = 5$

$\qquad h \longrightarrow 20\%$ decrease $h = 4$

$\qquad V = \pi r^2 = 25 \times 4 \times \pi = 100\pi$

$\dfrac{100\pi - 80\pi}{80\pi} = \dfrac{1}{4} = 25\%$ increase

Correct Answer : C

33. $\left(\dfrac{120}{60} + \dfrac{80}{60}\right) t = 360$

$\qquad \left(\dfrac{200}{60}\right) t = 360$

$\qquad \dfrac{10t}{3} = 360$

$\qquad \dfrac{t}{3} = 36$, $t = 108$

Correct Answer : C

34. $\quad \dfrac{a^{2m}}{a^{22}} = a^{18}$ Use the exponent division rule.

$a^{2m-22} = a^{18}$ Since base are same powers must be same to

$2m - 22 = 18$

$\qquad 2m = 18 + 22$

$\qquad 2m = 40$

$\qquad m = 20$

$\qquad a^{3n} = a^{45}$, $3n = 45$

$\qquad n = 15$

$\qquad m \cdot n = 20 \cdot 15 = 300$

Correct Answer : B

35. $\dfrac{\text{ratio of circumference}}{\text{ratio of arc}} = \dfrac{2\pi r}{\pi r^2}$

$\qquad\qquad = \dfrac{2\pi r}{\pi r^2} = \dfrac{2}{3}$

$\qquad \dfrac{2r}{r^2} = \dfrac{2}{3}$

$\qquad \dfrac{2}{r} = \dfrac{2}{3} \quad r = 3$

Correct Answer : 3

36. $2^x \cdot 2^x \cdot 2^x \cdot 2^x = 64^2 \longrightarrow$ Use exponent multiply rule.

$2^{x+x+x+x} = (2^6)^2$

$2^{4x} = 2^{12} \longrightarrow 4x = 12$, $x = 3$

Correct Answer : 3

37. $3^y + 3^y + 3^y = 81^2$

$3^y (1+1+1) = 81^2$

$3^y \cdot 3^1 = (3^4)^2$

$3^{y+1} = 3^8$

$y + 1 = 8$, $y = 7$

Correct Answer : 7

38. If $x = 7y$ and $\dfrac{x}{2} - \dfrac{y}{3} = 57$,

$\dfrac{7y}{2} - \dfrac{y}{3} = 57$ (find LCD)

$\dfrac{21y}{6} - \dfrac{2y}{6} = 57$ (cross multiply)

$21y - 2y = 6 \cdot 57$

$19y = 342$

$y = 18$

Correct Answer : 18

REFERENCE SHEET

Directions

For each question from 1–15, solve each problem, choose the best answer from the choices provided, and fill in the corresponding bubble on your answer sheet.

- For questions 16 to 20, solve the problem and enter your answer in the grid on the answer sheet.
- Refer to the directions before question 18 for how to enter your answers in the grid. You may use any available space for scratch work.

REFERENCE

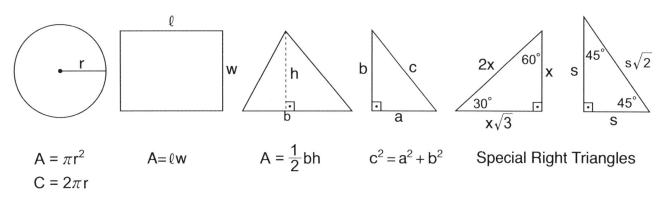

$A = \pi r^2$ $A = \ell w$ $A = \frac{1}{2} bh$ $c^2 = a^2 + b^2$ Special Right Triangles

$C = 2\pi r$

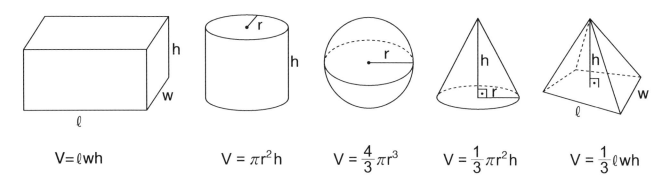

$V = \ell wh$ $V = \pi r^2 h$ $V = \frac{4}{3}\pi r^3$ $V = \frac{1}{3}\pi r^2 h$ $V = \frac{1}{3}\ell wh$

The number of degrees in a circle is 360.

The number of radians in a circle is 2π.

The sum of the measures in degrees of the angles of a triangle is 180.

1.

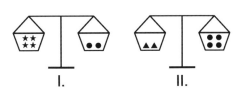

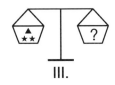

According to the diagram, which group of weights from figures I and II are equal to the weight of the question mark?

A) ● ● ●

B) ● ●

C) ● ● ▲

D) ● ● ★

2. Simplify $\dfrac{x^2y + xy^2 - xy}{x^2 + xy - x}$

A) x

B) y

C) 2xy

D) –x

3. The tree grows everyday at $\sqrt{x}$ cm.

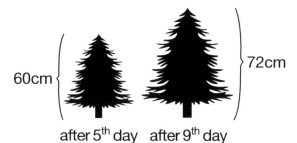

after 5th day   after 9th day

What is the height of the tree after the 15th day?

A) 80cm

B) 90cm

C) 100cm

D) 120cm

4. $\dfrac{x+3}{4} - \dfrac{x}{3} = \dfrac{3}{2}$, find the value of x.

A) –3

B) –6

C) –9

D) –12

5. If y varies inversely as x and x = 8 when y = 6, find y when x = 10.

A) 2.8

B) 3.8

C) 4.8

D) 5.8

American Math Academy

130

6. $\sqrt[2]{x+16}+\sqrt[2]{x}=8$, then x can be which of the following?

A) 3

B) 5

C) 7

D) 9

7. How many solutions does the system of equations shown below have?

$$2x = y + 4$$
$$4x - 5y = 8$$

A) Zero

B) 1

C) 2

D) Many/infinity

8. Simplify $\sqrt{27}-\sqrt{81}+\sqrt{243}$.

A) $3\sqrt{3}-9$

B) $6\sqrt{3}-9$

C) $9\sqrt{3}-9$

D) $12\sqrt{3}-9$

9. If $a=\sqrt{3}$ and $b=\sqrt{2}$ then find $\dfrac{a}{b}-\dfrac{b}{a}$.

A) $\dfrac{\sqrt{6}}{6}$

B) $\dfrac{1}{\sqrt{5}}$

C) $\dfrac{1}{\sqrt{3}}$

D) $\dfrac{1}{\sqrt{2}}$

10. The function $f(x) = (x-3)(x-5)(x+8)$ will intersect the x–axis how many times?

A) 0

B) 1

C) 2

D) 3

11. If x is a positive integer and $x^2 + x - 12 = 0$, what is the value of $x + 3$?

A) 3

B) 6

C) 9

D) 12

American Math Academy

12. In a right triangle, the cosine of angle B is $\frac{3}{5}$ and the sine of angle B is $\frac{4}{5}$.
What is the ratio of the longest side to the shortest side?

A) $\frac{4}{3}$

B) $\frac{4}{5}$

C) $\frac{3}{4}$

D) $\frac{5}{3}$

13. Suppose that x is an integer such that $\frac{x}{3}$ is 6 greater than $\frac{x}{4}$. Which of the following is the value of x?

A) 24

B) 36

C) 72

D) 96

14. Mr. Johnson gave the following list of numbers to his class. He asked the class to find all of the composite numbers in the list.

3, 4, 7, 11, 14, 19, 21, 33

Which of these shows all of the composite numbers in the list?

A) 3, 7, 11, 19

B) 4, 14, 21, 33

C) 4, 19, 21, 33

D) 4, 11, 21, 33

15.

1st basket   2nd basket   3rd basket

There are three baskets given above, and they have three kinds of squares.

The sequence of the weight of baskets is 1st > 2nd > 3rd. Which of the following statement is true?

(x = x's weight, y = y's weight, z = z's weight)

A) x > y > z

B) x > z > y

C) y > x > z

D) y > z > x

American Math Academy

16. If $4a + 5b = 16$ and $a = 3$ then find b?

17. If 6 is one of the solutions of the equation $x^2 - 3ax - 24 = 0$, what is the value of a?

18. For the function below, m>0 is a constant and f(2)=20. What is the value of f(5)?

$$f(x) = mx^2 - 4$$

19. In the following circle, O is the center of circle. What is the value of x?

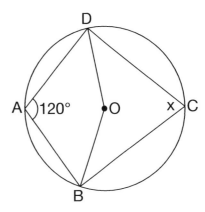

20. If the following polynomial P(x) is divisible by x+1 then find the remainder.

$$P(x) = x^{2018} + x^{2019} + x^{2020}$$

American Math Academy

PRACTICE TEST V ANSWER SHEET
NO CALCULATOR SECTION

1. Ⓐ Ⓑ Ⓒ Ⓓ   6. Ⓐ Ⓑ Ⓒ Ⓓ   11. Ⓐ Ⓑ Ⓒ Ⓓ
2. Ⓐ Ⓑ Ⓒ Ⓓ   7. Ⓐ Ⓑ Ⓒ Ⓓ   12. Ⓐ Ⓑ Ⓒ Ⓓ
3. Ⓐ Ⓑ Ⓒ Ⓓ   8. Ⓐ Ⓑ Ⓒ Ⓓ   13. Ⓐ Ⓑ Ⓒ Ⓓ
4. Ⓐ Ⓑ Ⓒ Ⓓ   9. Ⓐ Ⓑ Ⓒ Ⓓ   14. Ⓐ Ⓑ Ⓒ Ⓓ
5. Ⓐ Ⓑ Ⓒ Ⓓ   10. Ⓐ Ⓑ Ⓒ Ⓓ   15. Ⓐ Ⓑ Ⓒ Ⓓ

16. [grid-in answer grid]

17. [grid-in answer grid]

18. [grid-in answer grid]

19. [grid-in answer grid]

20. [grid-in answer grid]

REFERENCE SHEET

Directions

For each question from 1 to 34, solve each problem, choose the best answer from the choices provided, and fill in the corresponding bubble on your answer sheet.

- For questions 35 and 38, solve the problem and enter your answer in the grid on the answer sheet.
- Refer to the directions before question 35 for how to enter your answers in the grid. You may use any available space for scratch work.

REFERENCE

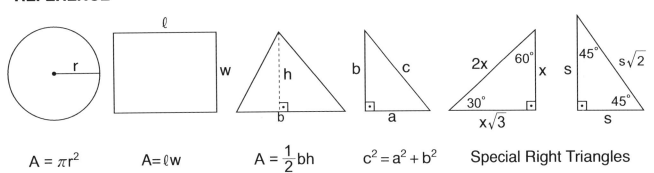

$A = \pi r^2$ $\qquad$ $A = \ell w$ $\qquad$ $A = \dfrac{1}{2}bh$ $\qquad$ $c^2 = a^2 + b^2$ $\qquad$ Special Right Triangles

$C = 2\pi r$

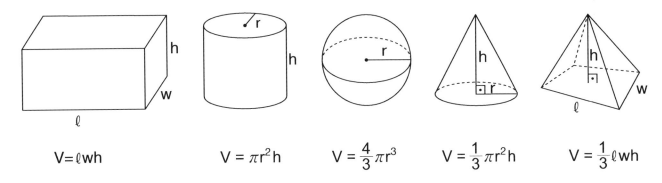

$V = \ell wh$ $\qquad$ $V = \pi r^2 h$ $\qquad$ $V = \dfrac{4}{3}\pi r^3$ $\qquad$ $V = \dfrac{1}{3}\pi r^2 h$ $\qquad$ $V = \dfrac{1}{3}\ell wh$

The number of degrees in a circle is 360.

The number of radians in a circle is 2π.

The sum of the measures in degrees of the angles of a triangle is 180.

1. What are the zeros of the function $f(x) = x^3 + 6x^2 + 9x$?

   A) 0, 2

   B) 0, −2

   C) 0, 3

   D) 0, −3

2. If x is a positive real number and $x - 2\sqrt{x} - 3 = 0$ then find $\dfrac{x}{x-1}$

   A) $\dfrac{1}{2}$

   B) $\dfrac{1}{4}$

   C) $\dfrac{9}{8}$

   D) $\dfrac{5}{3}$

3. The sum of five consecutive positive integers is 75. What is the greatest possible value of one of these integers?

   A) 13

   B) 15

   C) 17

   D) 27

4. If the ratio of $\dfrac{1}{3} : \dfrac{1}{b}$ is equal to $\dfrac{1}{18} : \dfrac{1}{12}$, what is the value of b?

   A) 9

   B) $\dfrac{9}{2}$

   C) $\dfrac{2}{9}$

   D) 2

5. If $3^{2x-4} = 27^{x-6}$, then what is the value of x?

   A) 12

   B) 14

   C) 16

   D) 18

6. For a > 5, which of the following is equivalent to

   $$\dfrac{1}{\dfrac{1}{x+3} + \dfrac{1}{x+5}} = ?$$

   A) $\dfrac{2x+8}{x^2+8x+15}$

   B) $\dfrac{x^2+8x+15}{2x+8x}$

   C) $\dfrac{2x+8}{x^2-8x+15}$

   D) $x^2+8x+15$

7. Which of the following complex number is equivalent to $\left(\dfrac{1+i}{1-i}\right)^{2020}$?

A) 1

B) −1

C) i

D) −i

8. The following chart show market stock in supermarkets which buy tea, coffee, soda and water after they sell them. Their prices are given in the chart.

	Cost	Sale
Tea	20	25
Coffee	12	18
Soda	20	24
Water	90	120

Which product has the highest rate of profit?

A) Tea

B) Coffee

C) Soda

D) Water

American Math Academy

9. Φ and $\oplus$ are functions on real numbers.

$$x\Phi y = \frac{x^2+y}{4} \text{ and } x\oplus y = \frac{3xy}{5}$$

$(2\Phi 1)\oplus(3\Phi 1) = ?$

A) $\dfrac{25}{4}$

B) $\dfrac{27}{4}$

C) $\dfrac{15}{8}$

D) $\dfrac{17}{2}$

10.

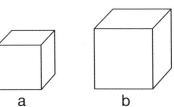

a	b	c
I.	II.	III.

There are three cubes given above. Their side length is given under the cubes. 'I' is a, 'II' is b, 'III' is c. Their volumes are V_a, V_b, and V_c.

$$c = 2b = 3a$$

$\dfrac{1}{V_a}+\dfrac{1}{V_b}+\dfrac{1}{V_c}=\dfrac{1}{6}$, then find volume of $V_c = ?$

A) 216

B) 125

C) 64

D) 27

11. The table below shows the results of a survey on how students get to school. A circle graph is to be used to display the data. What percent of the graph represents the car transportation?

Number of Students	Transportation
90	School bus
60	Car
10	Walk
40	Bike

A) 30%

B) 35%

C) 40%

D) 45%

12. If $2^{4a} = \dfrac{32}{2^a}$, then find the value of a.

A) 0

B) 1

C) 2

D) 3

13. $x \triangle y = \begin{cases} y^2 - x \,, & x \le y \\ \dfrac{-y}{3} \,, & x > y \end{cases}$

What is the solution of $(-4) \triangle \left| \dfrac{1}{4} \triangle (-3) \right| = ?$

A) 2

B) 3

C) 4

D) 5

14. Which of following could be a value of k in the following equation?

$$2k^2 - 3k + 1 = 0$$

A) 0

B) 1

C) 2

D) 3

15. On the xy coordinate grid, a line K contains the points (2, 3) and (−2, 7). If the line K is perpendicular to L at (3, 1), which of following is the equation of the line L?

A) $y = x - 2$

B) $y = -x + 4$

C) $y = x + 4$

D) $y = 2x - 4$

American Math Academy

16. What is the solution of the following system of equations?

$$3y = 6 + 4x$$
$$y = 8 - 2x$$

A) (1, 4)

B) (1.8, 4.4)

C) (2, 4)

D) (−1.8, 4)

17. If $6x = 8y + 10$ and $x - 3y = -5$ then what is the value of $\frac{y}{2}$?

A) 2

B) 3

C) 4

D) 6

18. What is the one possible value of $x - y$?

$$\frac{6}{8} < \frac{x}{2} - \frac{2y}{4} < \frac{3}{2}$$

A) 1

B) 2

C) 3

D) 4

19.

$$x = \$7 + 5k$$
$$y = \$5.5 + 10k$$

In above equation, x represents the price in dollars of apple juice and y represents the price in dollars of orange juice at the farmer's market and k is the same amount per week. What is the price of apple juice when it's the same as the price of orange juice?

A) $5

B) $6

C) $6.5

D) $8.5

20. Melisa is planning to register for fitness center training, and the center training monthly fee of $25 and $5 per hour for time training. Which of following functions gives Melisa the cost, in dollars, for a monthly fee in which she spends x hours training?

A) $F(x) = 5x$

B) $F(x) = 25x$

C) $F(x) = 5 + 25x$

D) $F(x) = 25 + 5x$

21. If the center of a circle is at (3, 6), and the radius of the circle is 4, what is the equation of that circle?

A) $(x - 3)^2 + (y - 6)^2 = 4$

B) $(x - 3)^2 + (y - 6)^2 = 8$

C) $(x - 3)^2 + (y - 6)^2 = 16$

D) $(x - 6)^2 + (y - 3)^2 = 4$

22. $P(x) = 3x^3 - 7x^2 + 2$ and $Q(x) = 2x^3 + 2x^2 + 5$ Then find $P(x) - Q(x)$.

A) $x^3 - 9x^2 - 3$

B) $x^3 + 9x^2 - 3$

C) $x^3 - 9x^2 + 7$

D) $x^3 - 2x^2 - 7$

23. $x \neq 0$, and $(x + y)^2 = (x - 2y)^2$

What is the value of $\dfrac{x}{y} + \dfrac{y}{x} = ?$

A) 2

B) 3

C) $\dfrac{5}{2}$

D) $\dfrac{3}{2}$

24. If x > 0 what is the value of x in $|2x - 3| = 7$?

A) −2

B) 2

C) 4

D) 5

25. If ab < 0 and b > 0 then which of following must be true?

A) a < 0

B) b < 0

C) a > 0

D) a = 0

26. The linear function g (x) is shown in the table below. Which of following defines g (x)?

x	g(x)
1	15
2	17
3	19

A) 2x + 10

B) 2x + 13

C) 2x − 13

D) 2x + 5

27. For what value of x is the equation $x^2 - 3x - 5 = 0$ true?

A) $\dfrac{3 \pm \sqrt{29}}{2}$

B) $\dfrac{-1 \pm \sqrt{19}}{2}$

C) $\dfrac{-3 \pm \sqrt{26}}{4}$

D) $\dfrac{-3 \pm \sqrt{29}}{6}$

28. The temperature in Celsius (C°) in the first week of October was as follow:

25C°, 21C°, 20C°, 25C°, 23C°, 14C°, 32C°

What is the mode of the temperatures for the first week of October?

A) 20C°

B) 21C°

C) 23C°

D) 25C°

29. $\tan x + \dfrac{\cos x}{1 + \sin x}$ what is the simplest form of the given equation?

A) secx

B) cosecx

C) cotx

D) $\sin^2 x$

30. Which of the following parabola functions could represent the graph in the picture?

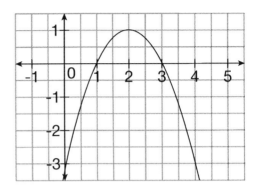

A) $f(x) = -x^2 + 4x + 3$

B) $f(x) = -x^2 - 4x + 3$

C) $f(x) = -x^2 - 4x - 3$

D) $f(x) = -x^2 + 4x - 3$

31. Which of the following complex numbers are equivalent to $\dfrac{a - bi}{a + bi}$?

A) $\dfrac{a^2 - 2abi + b^2}{a^2 + b^2}$

B) $a^2 + b^2$

C) $\dfrac{a^2 - 2abi + b^2}{a^2 - b^2}$

D) $\dfrac{a^2 - 2abi - b^2}{a^2 + b^2}$

American Math Academy

32.

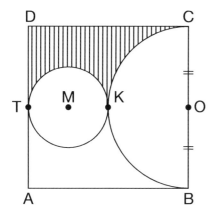

In the following figures, M and O are center of circles, ABCD is a square and AB = 4 feet.

What is the area of the shaded part?

A) $8 - \dfrac{3\pi}{2}$

B) $4 - \dfrac{3\pi}{2}$

C) $\dfrac{3\pi}{2} - 2$

D) $\dfrac{3\pi}{2}$

33.

$$\left| \frac{2x}{3} - 4 \right| < 12$$

What is a possible value of x in the above inequality?

A) −12

B) −5

C) 24

D) 25

34. $\dfrac{2a-3}{a-2} - 4 = \dfrac{3}{a-2}$, find the value of a

A) 1

B) 3

C) 4

D) 2

35. If $x^2 + 2x - 15 = (x - a)(x + b)$ for all values of x, what is the value of a · b?

A) 12

B) 15

C) 18

D) 21

American Math Academy

36. In the following figure, O is the center of the circle and the radius is 4 cm. Find the length of arc AB.

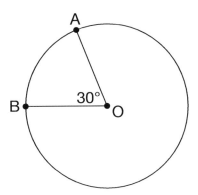

A) $\frac{2}{3}\pi$

B) $\frac{3}{2}\pi$

C) 3π

D) 2π

37. If $x^2 + 12x - 13 = 0$ and $x > 0$, what is the value of $x + 10$?

38. $6x - ay + 12 = 0$, if the slope of the equation is $\frac{1}{3}$, what is the value of a?

American Math Academy

PRACTICE TEST V ANSWER SHEET
CALCULATOR SECTION

1. Ⓐ Ⓑ Ⓒ Ⓓ   13. Ⓐ Ⓑ Ⓒ Ⓓ   24. Ⓐ Ⓑ Ⓒ Ⓓ
2. Ⓐ Ⓑ Ⓒ Ⓓ   14. Ⓐ Ⓑ Ⓒ Ⓓ   25. Ⓐ Ⓑ Ⓒ Ⓓ
3. Ⓐ Ⓑ Ⓒ Ⓓ   15. Ⓐ Ⓑ Ⓒ Ⓓ   26. Ⓐ Ⓑ Ⓒ Ⓓ
4. Ⓐ Ⓑ Ⓒ Ⓓ   16. Ⓐ Ⓑ Ⓒ Ⓓ   27. Ⓐ Ⓑ Ⓒ Ⓓ
5. Ⓐ Ⓑ Ⓒ Ⓓ   17. Ⓐ Ⓑ Ⓒ Ⓓ   28. Ⓐ Ⓑ Ⓒ Ⓓ
6. Ⓐ Ⓑ Ⓒ Ⓓ   18. Ⓐ Ⓑ Ⓒ Ⓓ   29. Ⓐ Ⓑ Ⓒ Ⓓ
7. Ⓐ Ⓑ Ⓒ Ⓓ   19. Ⓐ Ⓑ Ⓒ Ⓓ   30. Ⓐ Ⓑ Ⓒ Ⓓ
8. Ⓐ Ⓑ Ⓒ Ⓓ   20. Ⓐ Ⓑ Ⓒ Ⓓ   31. Ⓐ Ⓑ Ⓒ Ⓓ
9. Ⓐ Ⓑ Ⓒ Ⓓ   21. Ⓐ Ⓑ Ⓒ Ⓓ   32. Ⓐ Ⓑ Ⓒ Ⓓ
10. Ⓐ Ⓑ Ⓒ Ⓓ   22. Ⓐ Ⓑ Ⓒ Ⓓ   33. Ⓐ Ⓑ Ⓒ Ⓓ
11. Ⓐ Ⓑ Ⓒ Ⓓ   23. Ⓐ Ⓑ Ⓒ Ⓓ   34. Ⓐ Ⓑ Ⓒ Ⓓ
12. Ⓐ Ⓑ Ⓒ Ⓓ

35. 36. 37. 38.

PRACTICE TEST V
NO CALCULATOR SECTION ANSWER KEY

1)	A
2)	B
3)	B
4)	C
5)	C
6)	D
7)	B
8)	D
9)	A
10)	D
11)	B
12)	D
13)	C
14)	B
15)	B
16)	0.8 or 4/5
17)	2/3
18)	146
19)	60°
20)	1

1. $4\star = 2\bullet = $ I. $2\star = \bullet$

$2\blacktriangle = 4\bullet = $ II. $\blacktriangle = \bullet$

III. $\blacktriangle\star\star = \bullet\bullet\bullet$

Correct Answer : A

2. $\dfrac{x^2y + xy^2 - xy}{x^2 + xy - x}$

$= \dfrac{xy(x + y - 1)}{x(x + y - 1)}$

$= \dfrac{xy}{x} = y$

Correct Answer : B

3. $9 - 5 = 4\,\text{days}$

$4\sqrt{x} = 72cm - 60cm$

$4\sqrt{x} = 12cm$

$\sqrt{x} = 3cm \quad x = 9cm^2$

After 15th day's:

$= 60 + (15 - 5)\sqrt{9}$

$= 60 + 10\sqrt{9}$

$= 60 + 10 \cdot 3$

$= 60 + 30$

$= 90$

Correct Answer : B

4. $\dfrac{x + 3}{4} - \dfrac{x}{3} = \dfrac{3}{2}$ (Find LCD)

$\dfrac{3(x + 3)}{4 \cdot 3} - \dfrac{x(4)}{3(4)} = \dfrac{3(6)}{2(6)}$

$\dfrac{3x + 9}{12} - \dfrac{4x}{12} = \dfrac{18}{12}$

$3x + 9 - 4x = 18$

$-x + 9 = 18$

$-x = 9$

$x = -9$

Correct Answer : C

5. Inverse Variation: $y.x = k$

$6 \cdot 8 = k$

$48 = k$

$yx = k$

$y \cdot 10 = 48$

$y = 4.8$

Correct Answer : C

6. From the all choices x can be D (x = 9)

$\sqrt[2]{x + 16} + \sqrt[2]{x} = 8$

$\sqrt[2]{9 + 16} + \sqrt[2]{9} = 8$

$\sqrt[2]{25} + \sqrt[2]{9} = 8$

$5 + 3 = 8$

$8 = 8$

Correct Answer : D

American Math Academy

7. $-10x + 5y = -20$

$+ \quad \underline{4x - 5y = 8}$

$\qquad -6x = -12$

$\qquad\quad x = 2$

$4(2) - 5y = 8$

$\quad 8 - 5y = 8$

$\quad\;\; -5y = 0$

$\qquad\;\; y = 0$

Correct Answer : B

8. $= \sqrt{27} - \sqrt{81} + \sqrt{243}$

$= 3\sqrt{3} - 9 + 9\sqrt{3}$

$= 12\sqrt{3} - 9$

Correct Answer : D

9. $a = \sqrt{3}$ and $b = \sqrt{2}$, then

$\dfrac{a}{b} - \dfrac{b}{a} = \dfrac{\sqrt{3}}{\sqrt{2}} - \dfrac{\sqrt{2}}{\sqrt{3}} = \dfrac{\sqrt{3}(\sqrt{3})}{\sqrt{2}(\sqrt{3})} - \dfrac{\sqrt{2}(\sqrt{2})}{\sqrt{3}(\sqrt{2})}$

$= \dfrac{\sqrt{9}}{\sqrt{6}} - \dfrac{\sqrt{4}}{\sqrt{6}} = \dfrac{3}{\sqrt{6}} - \dfrac{2}{\sqrt{6}} = \dfrac{1}{\sqrt{6}} = \dfrac{\sqrt{6}}{6}$

Correct Answer : A

10. $f(x) = (x - 3)(x - 5)(x + 8)$

$x - 3 = 0, x = 3$

$x - 5 = 0, x = 5$

$x + 8 = 0, x = -8$

Correct Answer : D

11. $x^2 + x - 12 = 0$

$(x + 4)(x - 3) = 0$

$x = -4$ or $x = 3$ since x is positive integer x can be only 3.

$x + 3 = 3 + 3 = 6$

Correct Answer : B

12. $\text{Cosine B} = \dfrac{\text{adjacent}}{\text{hypotenuse}} = \dfrac{3}{5}$

$\text{Sine B} = \dfrac{\text{opposite}}{\text{hypotenuse}} = \dfrac{4}{5}$

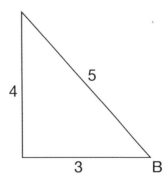

Ratio of the largest side to the shortest side

$= \dfrac{5}{3}$, or 5 to 3.

Correct Answer : D

13. $\dfrac{x}{3} = \dfrac{x}{4} + 6$

$\dfrac{x}{3} - \dfrac{x}{4} = 6$

$\dfrac{4x}{12} - \dfrac{3x}{12} = 6$

$\dfrac{x}{12} = 6$

$x = 6 \cdot 12$

$x = 72$

Correct Answer : C

14. All composite numbers: 4, 14, 21, 33

Correct Answer : B

15. 1st basket = 2x + y

2nd basket = y + 2z

3rd basket = 2y + z

2x + y > y + 2z and y + 2z > 2y + z

x > z   x > z > y

Correct Answer : B

16. 4a + 5b = 16 and a = 3

$4 \cdot 3 + 5b = 16$

$12 + 5b = 16$

$5b = 16 - 12$

$5b = 4$

$b = \dfrac{4}{5} = 0.8$

Correct Answer : 0.8 or 4/5

17. $x^2 - 3ax - 24 = 0$, since 6 is one of the solutions of the equation that means x can be 6.

$6^2 - 3a(6) - 24 = 0$

$36 - 18a - 24 = 0$

$12 - 18a = 0$

$a = \dfrac{12}{18} = \dfrac{2}{3}$ or 2/3

Correct Answer : 2/3

18. $f(2) = 20$

$f(x) = mx^2 - 4$

$f(2) = 2^2 \cdot m - 4$

$20 = 4m - 4$

$20 + 4 = 4m$

$24 = 4m$

$6 = m$

$f(x) = 6x^2 - 4$

$f(5) = 6 \cdot 5^2 - 4$

$f(5) = 6 \cdot 25 - 4$

$f(5) = 150 - 4$

$f(5) = 146$

Correct Answer : 146

American Math Academy

19.

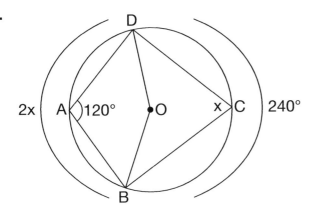

$\text{ArcBCD} = 240°$

$\text{ArcBCD} = 2x$

$2x + 240° = 360°$

$2x = 120°$

$x = 60°$

Correct Answer : 60°

American Math Academy

20. If P(x) is divisible by x+1, then x + 1 = 0, x = −1

$P(-1) = (-1)^{2018} + (-1)^{2019} + (-1)^{2020}$

$P(-1) = 1 - 1 + 1$

$P(-1) = 1$

Correct Answer : 1

PRACTICE TEST V
CALCULATOR SECTION ANSWER KEY

1)	D		20)	D
2)	C		21)	C
3)	C		22)	A
4)	D		23)	C
5)	B		24)	D
6)	B		25)	A
7)	A		26)	B
8)	B		27)	A
9)	C		28)	D
10)	A		29)	A
11)	A		30)	D
12)	B		31)	D
13)	D		32)	A
14)	B		33)	B
15)	A		34)	A
16)	B		35)	B
17)	A		36)	A
18)	B		37)	11
19)	D		38)	18

PRACTICE TEST V
CALCULATOR SECTION SOLUTIONS

1. $f(x) = x^3 + 6x^2 + 9x$

$x^3 + 6x^2 + 9x = 0$

$x(x^2 + 6x + 9) = 0$

$x(x + 3)^2 = 0$

$x = 0$ or $x = -3$

Correct Answer : D

2.

$x - 2\sqrt{x} - 3 = 0$

$x - 3 = (2\sqrt{x})^2$

$(x - 3)^2 = (\sqrt{4x})^2$

$(x - 3)^2 = 4x$

$x^2 - 6x + 9 = 4x$

$x^2 - 6x - 4x + 9 = 0$

$x^2 - 10x + 9 = 0$

$(x - 9) \cdot (x - 1) = 0$

$x = 9$ or $x = 1$ (x cannot be 1)

$\dfrac{x}{x-1} = \dfrac{9}{8}$

Correct Answer : C

3. The sum of five consecutive positive integers are: $x + x + 1 + x + 2 + x + 3 + x + 4 = 75$

$5x + 10 = 75$

$5x = 65$

$x = 13$

Greatest one: $x + 4 = 13 + 4 = 17$

Correct Answer : C

4. If the ratio of $\dfrac{1}{3} : \dfrac{1}{b}$ is equal to $\dfrac{1}{18} : \dfrac{1}{12}$

$\dfrac{1}{3} \cdot \dfrac{b}{1} = \dfrac{1}{18} \cdot \dfrac{12}{1}$

$\dfrac{b}{3} = \dfrac{12}{18}$

$b = \dfrac{3 \cdot 12}{18}$

$b = 2$

Correct Answer : D

5. $3^{2x-4} = 27^{x-6}$

$3^{2x-4} = 3^{3x-18}$

$2x - 4 = 3x - 18$

$-4 + 18 = 3x - 2x$

$14 = x$

Correct Answer : B

151

6.

$$\frac{1}{\dfrac{1}{x+3}+\dfrac{1}{x+5}}=$$

$$\frac{1}{\dfrac{(x+5)}{(x+3)\cdot(x+5)}+\dfrac{(x+3)}{(x+5)\cdot(x+3)}}=$$

$$\frac{1}{\dfrac{2x+8}{x^2+5x+3x+15}}=\frac{x^2+8x+15}{2x+8}$$

Correct Answer : B

7. $\left(\dfrac{1+i}{1-i}\right)^{2020}=\left(\dfrac{(1+i)(1+i)}{(1-i)(1+i)}\right)^{2020}=\left(\dfrac{2i}{2}\right)^{2020}$

$(i)^{2020}=(i^2)^{1010}=(-1)^{1010}=1$

Correct Answer : A

8. $\text{Tea}=\dfrac{25-20}{20}=\dfrac{5}{20}=25\%$

$\text{Coffee}=\dfrac{18-12}{12}=\dfrac{6}{12}=50\%$

$\text{Soda}=\dfrac{24-20}{20}=\dfrac{4}{20}=20\%$

$\text{Water}=\dfrac{120-90}{90}=\dfrac{30}{90}\approx 33\%$

the highest rate of profit is Coffee.

Correct Answer : B

9. $(2\Phi 1)=\dfrac{2^2+1}{4}=\dfrac{5}{4}$

$(3\Phi 1)=\dfrac{3^2+1}{4}=\dfrac{10}{4}$

$\left(\dfrac{5}{4}\oplus\dfrac{10}{4}\right)=\dfrac{3\cdot\dfrac{5}{4}\cdot\dfrac{10}{4}}{5}=\dfrac{15\cancel{0}}{8\cancel{0}}=\dfrac{15}{8}$

Correct Answer : C

10. Let $a=2k, b=4k, c=6k$

$$\frac{1}{8k^3}+\frac{1}{27k^3}+\frac{1}{216k^3}=\frac{1}{6}$$

$$\frac{27}{216k^3}+\frac{8}{216k^3}+\frac{1}{216k^3}=\frac{1}{6}$$

$$216k^3=6\cdot 36$$

$$216k^3=216$$

$$k^3=1$$

$$k=1$$

$$V_c=216k^3=216$$

Correct Answer : A

11. Percent of the graph represents the car transportation: $\dfrac{60}{200}=\dfrac{6}{20}$

$=\dfrac{6\cdot 5}{20\cdot 5}=\dfrac{30}{100}=30\%$

Correct Answer : A

12. $2^{4a} = \dfrac{32}{2^a}$

$2^{5a} = 2^5, a = 1$

Correct Answer : B

13. $\dfrac{1}{4} > -3$, then $\dfrac{-(-3)}{3} = 1$

$(-4) \triangle 1 \Longrightarrow -4 \leq 1$

$1^2 - (-4) = 5$

Correct Answer : D

14. $2k^2 - 3k + 1 = 0$

$(2k - 1)(k - 1) = 0$

$k = 1$ or $k = \dfrac{1}{2}$

Correct Answer : B

15. (2, 3) and (−2, 7).

Slope of line K $= \dfrac{y_2 - y_1}{x_2 - x_1} = \dfrac{7 - 3}{-2 - 2} = -\dfrac{4}{4} = 1$,

since line K and line L are perpendicular slope of L is 1.

$y = mx + b$, $y = x + b$

use (3, 1) to find b.

$1 = 3\,(1) + b$

$-2 = b$

$y = x - 2$

Correct Answer : B

16. $3y = 6 + 4x$ and $y = 8 - 2x$, then $3(8 - 2x) = 6 + 4x$.

$24 - 6x = 6 + 4x$

$24 - 6 = 4x + 6x$

$18 = 10x$

$1.8 = x$

$4.4 = y$

Correct Answer : B

17.

If $6x = 8y + 10$ and $x - 3y = -5$, then $x = 3y - 5$.

$6(3y - 5) = 8y + 10$

$18y - 30 = 8y + 10$

$18y - 8y = 30 + 10$

$10y = 40$

$y = 4$, then $\dfrac{y}{2} = \dfrac{4}{2} = 2$

Correct Answer : A

18. $\dfrac{6}{8} < \dfrac{x}{2} - \dfrac{2y}{4} < \dfrac{3}{2}$

$= \dfrac{6}{8} < \dfrac{4x}{8} - \dfrac{4y}{8} < \dfrac{12}{8}$

$6 < 4x - 4y < 12$

$\dfrac{6}{4} < x - y < \dfrac{12}{4}$

$\dfrac{3}{2} < x - y < 3$

One possible value of $x - y$ is 2.

Correct Answer : B

American Math Academy

19. $7 + 5k = 5.5 + 10k$

$\quad k = 0.3$

Price of orange juice

$\quad y = 5.5 + 10k$

$\quad y = 5.5 + 10 \cdot (0.3)$

$\quad y = 5.5 + 3$

$\quad y = 8.5$

Correct Answer : D

20. Monthly Fee = $25

$5 Per Hour

Monthly Spending x Hours

$F(x) = 25 + 5x$

Correct Answer : D

21. $(x - h)^2 + (y - k)^2 = r^2$

$\quad (x - 3)^2 + (y - 6)^2 = 16$

Correct Answer : C

22. $P(x) - Q(x) = (3x^3 - 7x^2 + 2) - (2x^3 + 2x^2 + 5)$

$\quad = x^3 - 9x^2 - 3$

Correct Answer : A

23. $\qquad (x + y)^2 = (x - 2y)^2$

$\quad x^2 + 2xy + y^2 = x^2 - 4xy + 4y^2$

$\qquad 6xy = 3y^2$

$\qquad 2x = y$

$\qquad \dfrac{x}{y} + \dfrac{y}{x} = \dfrac{x^2 + y^2}{xy}$

$\qquad\qquad = \dfrac{x^2 + 4x^2}{2x^2} = \dfrac{5}{2}.$

Correct Answer : C

24. $2x - 3 = \mp 7$

$\quad 2x - 3 = 7$

$\qquad 2x = 10$

$\qquad\quad x = 5$

$\qquad\quad$ or

$\quad 2x - 3 = -7$

$\quad 2x = -4 \quad , \quad x = -2$

since $x > 0$ then $x = 5$

Correct Answer : D

25. If $ab < 0$ and $b > 0$ then a must be negative $(a < 0)$.

Correct Answer : A

26. Linear function $g(x) = mx + b$

Slope $= \dfrac{y_2 - y_1}{x_2 - x_1} = \dfrac{17 - 15}{2 - 1} = \dfrac{2}{1} = 2$

$g(x) = 2x + b$, use any point from the table to find b.

$15 = 2(1) + b$

$15 - 2 = b$

$b = 13$

$g(x) = 2x + 13$

Correct Answer : B

27. $x^2 - 3x - 5 = 0$, Solve with a completing the square.

$x^2 - 3x = 5$

$\left(x - \dfrac{3}{2}\right)^2 - \dfrac{9}{4} = 5$

$\left(x - \dfrac{3}{2}\right)^2 = \dfrac{9}{4} + 5$

$\left(x - \dfrac{3}{2}\right)^2 = \dfrac{29}{4}$

$x - \dfrac{3}{2} = \pm\sqrt{\dfrac{29}{4}}$

$x = \dfrac{3 \pm \sqrt{29}}{2}$

Correct Answer : A

28. Mode: The mode is the most frequent value. From data the correct answer is $25C°$

Correct Answer : D

29. $\dfrac{\sin x}{\cos x} + \dfrac{\cos x}{1 + \sin x} = \dfrac{\sin x + \sin^2 x + \cos^2 x}{\cos x(1 + \sin x)}$

$= \dfrac{1 + \sin x}{\cos x(1 + \sin x)} = \dfrac{1}{\cos x} = \sec x$

Correct Answer : A

30. From the graph the Vertex Point is $(2,1)$.

$V(x) = a(x - h)^2 + k$

$V(x) = a(x - 2)^2 + 1$

From the graph you can use $(0, -3)$

$-3 = a(a - 2)^2 + 1$

$-3 = 4a + 1$

$-4 = 4a$, $a = -1$

$V(x) = -(x - 2)^2 + 1$

$V(x) = -(x^2 - 4x + 4) + 1$

$= -x^2 + 4x - 4 + 1$

$= -x^2 + 4x - 3$

Correct Answer : D

31. $\dfrac{a - bi}{a + bi} = \dfrac{(a - bi)(a - bi)}{(a + bi)(a - bi)}$

$= \dfrac{a^2 - abi - bai + b^2 i^2}{a^2 - b^2 i^2}$

$= \dfrac{a^2 - 2abi - b^2}{a^2 + b^2}$

Correct Answer : D

American Math Academy

155

32. $A(ABCD) = 4^2 = 16\text{ft}^2$

$A(TDCO) = 4 \cdot 2 = 8\text{ft}^2$

Area of small half circle $= \dfrac{\pi r^2}{2} = \dfrac{\pi}{2}$

Area of quarter of big circle $= \dfrac{\pi r^2}{2} = \dfrac{\pi \cdot 2^2}{4} = \pi$

Shaded area $= 8 - \left(\dfrac{\pi}{2} + \pi\right) = 8 - \dfrac{3\pi}{2}$

Correct Answer : A

33.

$$\left|\dfrac{2x}{3} - 4\right| < 12$$

$$-12 < \dfrac{2x}{3} - 4 < 12$$

$$\dfrac{2x}{3} < 16 \text{ or } \dfrac{2x}{3} > -8$$

$$x < 24 \text{ or } x > -12$$

$$-12 < x < 24$$

Correct Answer : B

34. $\dfrac{2a - 3 - 4a + 8}{a - 2} = \dfrac{3}{a - 2}$

$$-2a + 5 = 3$$

$$-2a = -2$$

$$a = 1$$

Correct Answer : A

35. $x^2 + 2x - 15 = (x - a)(x + b)$

$x^2 + 2x - 15 = x^2 + x(b - a) - ab$

$-15 = -ab$, then $ab = 15$

Correct Answer : B

36.

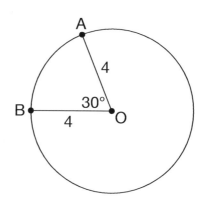

$\text{ArcAB} = \dfrac{2\pi r \alpha}{360}$

$$= \dfrac{2 \cdot \pi \cdot 4 \cdot 30}{360}$$

$$= \dfrac{2}{3}\pi$$

Correct Answer : A

American Math Academy

37. $x^2 + 12x - 13 = 0$

$(x + 13)(x - 1) = 0$

$x = -13$ and $x = 1$, since x is a positive integer x can be only 1.

$x + 10 = 10 + 1 = 11$

Correct Answer : 11

38. $6x - ay + 12 = 0$

$y = \dfrac{6x}{a} + \dfrac{12}{a}$, slope $= \dfrac{6}{a}$

$\dfrac{6}{a} = \dfrac{1}{3}$, $a = 18$

Correct Answer : 18

American Math Academy

Made in the USA
Lexington, KY
13 December 2019